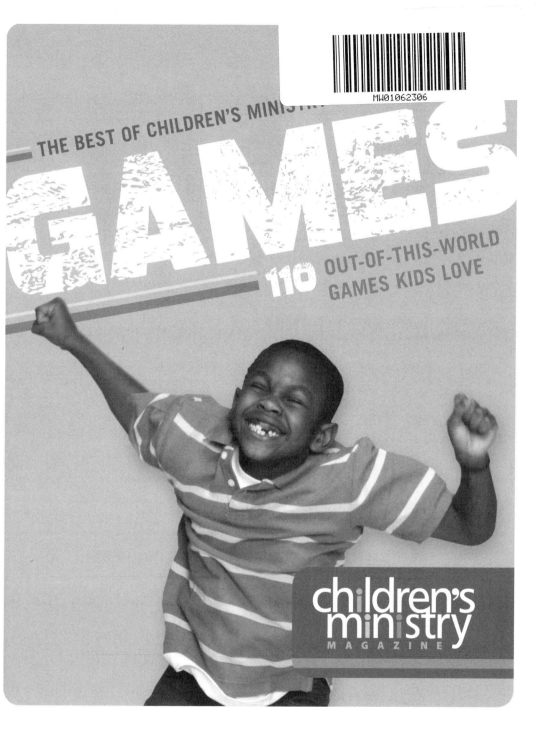

THE BEST OF CHILDREN'S MINISTRY

GAMES

110 OUT-OF-THIS-WORLD GAMES KIDS LOVE

children's ministry
MAGAZINE

Group

Loveland, Colorado | www.group.com

Group resources actually work!

This Group resource helps you focus on **"The 1 Thing®"**— a life-changing relationship with Jesus Christ. "The 1 Thing" incorporates our **R.E.A.L.** approach to ministry. It reinforces a growing friendship with Jesus, encourages long-term learning, and results in life transformation, because it's:

Relational
Learner-to-learner interaction enhances learning and builds Christian friendships.

Experiential
What learners experience through discussion and action sticks with them up to 9 times longer than what they simply hear or read.

Applicable
The aim of Christian education is to equip learners to be both hearers and doers of God's Word.

Learner-based
Learners understand and retain more when the learning process takes into consideration how they learn best.

The Best of Children's Ministry Magazine: GAMES
110 Out-of-This-World Games Kids Love

Credits

Editor: Laurie Copley
Quality Control Editor: Christine Yount Jones
Chief Creative Officer: Joani Schultz
Art Director: Josh Emrich
Cover Art Director/Designer: Josh Emrich
Assistant Art Director/Print Production Artist: Joyce Douglas
Photography: Rodney Stewart
Production Manager: Dodie Tipton

Library of Congress Cataloging-in-Publication Data
Best of Children's ministry magazine : games.
  p.   cm.
  Includes indexes.
  ISBN-13: 978-0-7644-3438-9 (alk. paper)
1. Games in Christian education. 2. Church work with children. 3. Bible games and puzzles. I. Group Publishing. II. Children's ministry.
BV1536.3.B47 2006
268'.432--dc22   2006026975

10 9 8 7 6 5 4 3 2   16 15 14 13 12 11 10 09 08 07
Printed in the United States of America.

THANKS TO OUR TALENTED AUTHORS!

Geoffrey Allan
Matt Augee
Patty Baker
Glynis Belec
Mary Vance Berlin
Rodney Bertholet
Mary Burman
Carolyn Caufman
Scott Cunningham
Mary J. Davis
Lynette Edmondson
Llona English
Nanette Goings
Donna Gossett
Sheila Halasz
Patty Harkiewicz
Deb Harrell
Margaret Hinchey
Mary Conley Holladay
Jennifer Hooks
Debra Jennings
Selma Johnson
Amy Jones
Christine Yount Jones
Carmen Kamrath
Janel Kauffman
Rebecca Kerr
Robyn Kundert
Rick Lawrence
Susan Lingo
Melodee Lovering
Dalinda Marshall
Brian Mason

Dwight Mix
Heather Monkmeyer
Jeff Moody
Lisa Nagy
Martin Nagy
Amy Nappa
Mike Nappa
Cindy Newell
Lori Haynes Niles
Walter Norvell
Debbie Trafton O'Neal
Nancy Paulson
CliffAnn Perry
Shannon Rayne
Lori Resch
Glenna Rufca
Jordan Sharp
Cindy Smith
Esther Stockwell
Nancy Tichy
Jan Tomlinson
Susan Turner
Heather Ward
Randy Warner
Deb Weaver
Jennifer Wilger
Joanne Wilson
Terry Vermillion
Mary G. Yates
Malinda Zellman

CONTENTS

GAMES FOR HIGH ENERGY 51

CONTENTS

GAMES FOR HIGH ENERGY continued

INDEX 121

INTRODUCTION

Kids love to play! But should playing games be part of the precious time you have to teach? Absolutely!

Kids remember what they do, so games are a perfect way to emphasize and help them remember the important Bible truths you teach.

That's why we've taken 110 of the best game ideas from Children's Ministry Magazine and put them all into one easy-to-use book. Gleaned from issues spanning the last 10 years, these creative games are not only fun to play, but easy to lead.

Children's ministry experts from all over the country have contributed these game ideas, so we know they work! A helpful index makes it possible to search by Scripture reference, and games are grouped in sections according to activity level. So finding the perfect game to play will be—well, child's play!

Use this collection of best game ideas:

- to plan games for your next special event,
- to fill in the gaps of your curriculum,
- as an instant resource when you need an instant game,
- to offer as a resource to help volunteers in their planning of events, and
- as an emergency resource when you need a fun and easy game idea.

Keep this book handy—you'll use it often! It's a game lifesaver for Sunday school, children's church, midweek programs, vacation Bible school, and camps.

Now go play!

GAMES FOR

LOW/MODERATE ENERGY

ANGER BUBBLES

Kids learn how quickly anger can bubble over.

WHAT YOU'LL NEED:

You'll need dishwashing liquid, a straw for each person, and 2 large bowls filled with water.

FOR EXTRA IMPACT:

- Read aloud **James 1:20,** and ask: Why do you think anger doesn't bring a "righteous life that God desires"? What would God have us do?

- Read aloud **Proverbs 15:1** and ask: How does a gentle answer turn away anger?

- Have kids mix paint with a small amount of water and bubble bath in a container and then use their straw to blow air into the mixture to create bubbles. Have kids write on a piece of paper, "'Be quick to listen, slow to speak and slow to become angry'—James 1:19." Kids can then place the paper over the bubbles to make a bubbly print.

DIRECTIONS

Form two groups. Designate one group as Group 1 and the other group as Group 2. Give each person a straw.

Say: Let's pretend this dishwashing liquid is "anger." I'm dropping one drop of anger in each bowl. Group 1, blow as quickly as you can to produce lots of bubbles. Group 2, blow as slowly as you can to produce the least number of bubbles.

Continue the game until bubbles are about to overflow the "quick-blowing" bowl. Exchange groups and repeat the game.

Read aloud **James 1:19**. Ask: What happened when you blew quickly? How was that bowl like or unlike someone who is quick to anger? What happened when you blew slowly? How is that like or unlike someone who is slow to anger? What happens when we quickly lose our temper? What makes you angry? What helps you keep from getting angry quickly?

BIBLE LOOK-UP

Here's a game that helps kids learn the books of the Bible, and it's a great energy release.

WHAT YOU'LL NEED:

You'll need a Bible, construction paper, scissors, pen, hole punch, tape, and ribbon.

FOR EXTRA IMPACT:

- Form groups of four, and give each group a set of index cards with a different Bible book name written on each one. Have kids work together to arrange the book names in order.

- Have groups race to see who can put the cards in order the fastest or race to see who can be the first group to divide the cards into Old Testament and New Testament books.

- Read aloud **2 Timothy 3:16**. Ask kids: Why is it important to read the Bible?

DIRECTIONS

Before class, write each Bible book name on a different piece of 3x10-inch construction paper. Punch a hole at the top of each paper, attach ribbon, and hang it from the ceiling.

Call out a book of the Bible, and have kids look for it on the ceiling. When they find it, they stand under it and point up. Call out the books in order or mixed up for added fun.

For a review game, play Name That Book. Give clues to a major event that occurs in a Bible book. When kids know which book the event or story comes from, they should stand under the book and point up.

BIBLE SMUGGLE

Kids learn about the importance of the Bible.

WHAT YOU'LL NEED:

You'll need a small Bible.

FOR EXTRA IMPACT:

- Read aloud **2 Timothy 3:14-17,** and ask kids: How does the Bible make us wise? What does it mean that "all Scripture is God-breathed"? Why does God want to equip us?

- Let kids each make a "Bible" snack. Spread softened cream cheese between two graham cracker halves, cover with chocolate frosting, then use a tube of white icing to write "Holy Bible" on the top.

ALLERGY ALERT

Be aware that some children have food allergies that can be dangerous. Know your children, and consult with parents about allergies their children may have. Also be sure to read food labels carefully as hidden ingredients can cause allergy-related problems.

DIRECTIONS

Form a circle with kids holding their hands behind their backs. Choose someone to be "It." Have It stand in the center of the circle. Hand a small Bible to one person in the circle. Have that person pass the Bible to someone else behind his or her back. Encourage kids to try to confuse the person in the middle so he or she doesn't know where the Bible is. Kids could pretend to pass the Bible back and forth.

After three minutes, have It guess who's holding the Bible. If caught, that person becomes It. If not, have It guess again. Play this game until children tire of it.

Then say: In some countries, it's against the law to have a Bible. So Christians smuggle the Bible into these countries. Many people risk their lives so people can have a Bible.

Ask: How did you feel when the Bible came to your hands? If it were against the law in our country to have a Bible, what would you do? What risks would you take to get the Bible to people who have no Bible? Why is the Bible important to our growth as Christians?

BIBLE-VERSE PUZZLE

Kids learn a scrambled Scripture verse.

WHAT YOU'LL NEED:

You'll need a Bible, pictures, paper, envelopes, glue, scissors, and a pen.

FOR EXTRA IMPACT:

- Have kids find partners and share their verses. Then trade puzzles, and play again.

- To make it even more difficult, partners can mix their puzzles together and then try to put each puzzle back together.

- Challenge kids to take their puzzles home to share with family members.

DIRECTIONS

Before class, glue a kid-friendly picture to a sheet of paper for each child. Print a Bible verse on the back of the paper. Then cut the picture into large, puzzle-piece shapes. Place the puzzle pieces in an envelope.

When children arrive, give them each a puzzle envelope and have them each put the puzzle together. After the picture puzzles are together, have kids turn over the puzzles and reassemble any scattered pieces. Help younger children read the verse on the back.

Not only will children have fun putting the puzzles together, they'll also learn a Bible verse.

BIBLE-VERSE VOLLEYBALL

Use this fun game to help your children memorize Scripture.

WHAT YOU'LL NEED:

You'll need a Bible, chalk, chalkboard, a table, and a balloon.

FOR EXTRA IMPACT:

- Use Scripture verses your class is currently studying, or use Bible verses such as **Exodus 20:12**; **Psalm 119:1**; **Matthew 7:7**; or **Galatians 5:22-23**.

- Have kids form teams of four and give each team a construction-paper "volleyball" with the Scripture verse written on it and cut into puzzle pieces. Team members will work together to construct the puzzle.

- Play Bible-Verse Volleyball in reverse using short Scripture verses that are familiar to the kids. Each time the balloon hits the floor, give kids one word of the Scripture verse and let them try to figure out the entire verse.

DIRECTIONS

Write a Bible verse on a chalkboard. Form two teams, and have teams stand on opposite sides of a table. Toss an inflated balloon to one team and have them "serve" it to the other team. Each team gets only three times to hit the balloon before hitting it back over the table.

If the balloon touches the floor, the team whose side the balloon is on must read the Bible verse together. Each time the verse is read, erase a word. Continue until one team has to say the entire verse from memory.

BLANKET VOLLEYBALL

Kids will love this team balancing act.

WHAT YOU'LL NEED:

You'll need a rope, 2 chairs, 2 small blankets or twin sheets, and several small foam-rubber balls.

FOR EXTRA IMPACT:

- On a piece of paper, have older kids each write: "'A friend loves at all times'— Proverbs 17:17." Then have kids write one thing they can do during the week to help their friends. Younger kids can draw pictures.

- Encourage kids to put their papers on their bedroom walls as a reminder to help their friends.

- Give kids cinnamon candy hearts. Remind them that friendship is sometimes difficult and wonderful, just like the candy hearts are spicy and sweet.

See page 12.

DIRECTIONS

Tie a rope to two chairs, and stretch it across your room. Form two teams, and have teams stand on opposite sides of the rope. Give each team a small blanket or twin sheet. Have team members hold the edges of their team's blanket.

Throw several small foam-rubber balls on one team's blanket. Have those team members work together to toss the balls from their blanket over the rope to the other blanket. Encourage kids on the receiving side to try to catch all the balls. Then have them toss the balls back to the other side.

Continue tossing several times or until children tire of this game. After the game, have children gather around you. Ask: When were you most successful at this game? How important is it for friends to help each other? How do you help your friends?

Say: **Proverbs 17:17** says that "a friend loves at all times." Ask: What does it mean to love at all times? When is it most difficult to love or help your friends? What's one way you can help a friend this week?

Say: Let's remember this week how important it is to help our friends.

LOW / MODERATE ENERGY

BOMBS AWAY

Kids love this wet reminder that God showers us with blessings.

WHAT YOU'LL NEED:

You'll need balloons, water, and towels.

FOR EXTRA IMPACT:

• Read aloud **Ezekiel 34:25-27,** and ask kids: Why does God shower us with his blessings?

• Write "God's Blessings" on uninflated balloons. Give kids each a balloon to take home and blow up when they need a reminder that God showers his blessings on us.

• Make a large paper tree, and put it on a bulletin board. Have kids write blessings they've received on construction paper leaves. Attach the leaves to the blessing tree.

DIRECTIONS

Before this game, fill small balloons with water, and tie them off. Take children outside, and have them sit in a tight circle on the ground. Tell children they must stay seated.

Have a group of adults gather around the children and throw the balloons straight up in the air over the circle. The children can try to catch the falling balloons, but they can't get up.

Usually the balloons will burst as the children try to catch them. If a child catches a balloon, he or she gets a free throw at an adult.

After the game, give kids towels to dry off. Encourage the children to remember that God showers us with blessings and good things. Talk about various ways God has showered them with his blessings.

CIRCLE PULL

Kids learn to work together in this challenging game.

WHAT YOU'LL NEED:

You'll need a large rope for every 10 kids.

FOR EXTRA IMPACT:

• Have kids play again, but instead of working together, have them race to see who can get up first. Ask: In which game was it easier to stand up? Explain. Why was it important to work together in the first game? What would happen if everyone fended for himself or herself all the time? Why does God want us to work together?

DIRECTIONS

Have children form groups of 10 or more. Have each group sit in a circle with kids' feet stretched out in the center of the circle. Tie the ends of a large rope together to make a huge loop. Place the rope loop inside the circle in front of kids' feet.

Have kids grab the rope with their hands and pull together at the same time. Kids must work together for everyone to stand up at the same time. Try until kids can do this together.

FOOD-TOWER FRENZY

Kids learn about building on a firm foundation.

WHAT YOU'LL NEED:

You'll need praise music and food service gloves (1 glove per child). For each team you'll need a plastic shower cap; a clean towel; plastic wrap; and snacks such as cookies, crackers, wafers, pretzels, and marshmallows.

FOR EXTRA IMPACT:

- Have kids form two teams, and let one team build a house with cards and the other team build a house with blocks.

- Read aloud **Matthew 7:24-27**, and ask kids: Which house was more like the house built on stone? on sand? Explain. Which house was our food tower most like? Explain.

- Read aloud **1 Corinthians 3:10-11**, and ask: Which foundation is Jesus most like? Explain.

ALLERGY ALERT
See page 12.

▶ DIRECTIONS

Form teams of four. Designate one child in each team as the Foundation. Have this child put on a plastic shower cap and lie on her back on a clean towel. Place plastic wrap over her forehead, and have her keep her face as level as possible. Give food-service gloves to the other kids. Play music for three minutes, and have the other team members attempt to stack as many snacks as possible on the foreheads of their team's Foundation. Use cookies, crackers, wafers, pretzels, and marshmallows as the snacks. Stop the music, and see which team built the tallest structure.

Judge the structures on height, number of snacks, and creativity. Declare all teams winners, and let the kids eat their creations.

Potential teaching aims: Tower of Babel, building a firm foundation, or discussion on food as a quality building material (not!).

FRIENDSHIP CIRCLE

This game will build children's self-esteem.

WHAT YOU'LL NEED:

You'll need 1 Hula-Hoop and 2 large jars. For each child, you'll need a Ping-Pong ball with his or her name written on it with a permanent marker.

FOR EXTRA IMPACT:

- Read aloud **Ecclesiastes 4:9-10,** and ask: Why do you think the Bible says that two are better than one? What are some ways that friends can help each other?

- Let kids use markers to decorate their Ping-Pong balls with happy faces to take home as reminders to be helpful friends.

DIRECTIONS

Place the Hula-Hoop on the floor in the center of the room. Have the children sit around the hoop. Place the balls in one jar.

Choose one child to draw a ball from the container. Put that ball in the second jar. Have the child who chose the ball step into the "Friendship Circle" and invite the child whose name is on the chosen ball to join him or her in the Friendship Circle.

After both children are in the circle, the first child tells three reasons the second child would be a good friend. The first child steps out of the circle and the second child draws another ball.

This process continues until every child has been in the Friendship Circle. There should be two children in the circle throughout the game. Continue this game until all the balls have been drawn.

HEAD POWER

Kids learn to cast their worries on God.

WHAT YOU'LL NEED:

You'll need a Bible and 5 books for each pair of kids.

FOR EXTRA IMPACT:

- Have kids each fold 8½x11-inch sheets of paper in half to make journals. Punch three holes in the folded edge with a hole punch, string with ribbon, and tie to secure the pages.

- Give kids Bibles, and have them write the following Scriptures in their books: **Psalm 27:1**; **Psalm 34:4**; **Psalm 34:7**; and **1 Peter 5:7**.

- Encourage kids to write their concerns and anxieties in their journals and then read the Scriptures to remind them to trust God and cast their worries on him.

DIRECTIONS

Have kids form pairs and sit on the floor facing their partner. Give each pair five books.

Say: Let's pretend these books are anxieties or things you worry about. Play Rock, Paper, Scissors with your partner. Scissors beats paper, paper beats rock, and rock beats scissors. If you lose, put a book on your head. If the book falls, add one more to your head. Play again until all the books are used.

Ask: How anxious did you feel during this game? Why? In real life, what is it like when anxieties or worries weigh you down?

Read aloud **1 Peter 5:7**. Have children each take a book and think about one worry they have. Have them one at a time lay that "worry" on the table as they silently commit to trust God in that area.

HIDE THE SIN

Kids learn that God doesn't want us to hide our sins.

WHAT YOU'LL NEED:

You'll need a Bible, masking tape, and a rock.

FOR EXTRA IMPACT:

- At the beginning of class, give kids each a large rock with *sin* written on it. Tell kids they have to carry the rock during class without putting it down.

- At the end of class, ask: What was it like carrying your rock around? Explain. How is this like or unlike what happens when we carry our sins and don't turn to Jesus for his forgiveness?

DIRECTIONS

Wrap masking tape around a rock, and write "sin" on it. Have children take turns holding the "sin" rock. Then have all the other kids close their eyes while one child hides it.

Once it's hidden, tell the other kids to search for and find the "sin" rock. After three or four times, have kids sit in a circle. Ask: What happened when we hid the "sin" rock?

Read aloud **Numbers 32:23**. Ask: What does this verse mean? Have you ever had a sin discovered even though you tried to hide it? What happened? Does God want us to try to hide our sins? What does God want us to do when we've sinned?

Have a child read aloud **1 John 1:9** while you use a marker to blot out the word *sin* on the rock. Lead children in a prayer of thanks for God's great forgiveness through Jesus Christ.

HOOP SHOOP

Kids love this hands-on game of Tag.

WHAT YOU'LL NEED:

You'll need 1 Hula-Hoop for every 5 players.

FOR EXTRA IMPACT:

- Have kids play again, but this time with only one player on the outside of the hoop. Have kids take turns so everyone has a try. Ask: Was it easier playing alone or with others? Explain.

- Read aloud **Ecclesiastes 4:10-12**. Ask: What do you think the Scripture means when it says a chord of three strands is not quickly broken?

- Let kids test the strength of one piece of string compared to three pieces of string woven together.

DIRECTIONS

Choose one player to be "It." Have "It" stand in the center of the Hula-Hoop and the other four players outside the circle. Have the four players alternate holding the Hula-Hoop first with one hand and then the other while "It" tries to tap a hand. The child who is "It" can pretend to be going for one hand and then tap another. The players outside the circle can pretend to switch hands or take their hands off the hoop entirely.

The game is over if players drop the hoop. Any player who is tapped becomes the new "It," and the game begins again.

Try this variation: Blindfold "It," and have players circle clockwise while they hold the hoop.

IN GOD'S IMAGE

Kids learn that God makes us special.

WHAT YOU'LL NEED:

You'll need a Bible.

FOR EXTRA IMPACT:

• Have kids each cut carboard into the shape of a hand-held-mirror and glue a piece of smooth foil onto the mirror for the "glass." Then write these words on the mirror's handle: "I'm made in God's image."

• Have real mirrors on hand, and let kids compare the image they see in the real mirror with the mirror they made. Ask: Which image is better? Why? Which is more like the image that God sees? Explain.

• Have kids sit in a circle and one at a time say something encouraging about the child to the right. Continue around the circle until everyone has had a turn. Then close in prayer, thanking God for making each of us in his image.

DIRECTIONS

Have kids form pairs, face their partners, and decide who'll be the Model and who'll be the Mirror. Have the Models move about as the Mirrors imitate their actions. After several minutes, have kids switch positions so the Model is now the Mirror.

Ask: How was this activity similar to or different from looking in a real mirror? What do you see when you look into a real mirror? How do you feel about what you see when you look into a real mirror? Explain.

Read aloud **Genesis 1:27** and **Psalm 139:13-16**. Ask: What does it mean to be created in the image of God? How does being created in the image of God make each of us special? What is one special quality God created in you that can't be seen in a mirror? (Have each child answer.)

LOW / MODERATE ENERGY

LENTEN SCAVENGER HUNT

This fun scavenger hunt helps kids dig into the Bible.

LOW / MODERATE ENERGY

WHAT YOU'LL NEED:

For each team, you'll need a Bible, paper, markers, and a copy of the scavenger list.

FOR EXTRA IMPACT:

- Have kids talk about what Jesus' death and resurrection means to them. Then have groups share their responses with the class.

- Give kids clay, and let them mold small pocket-size crosses to take home as keepsake reminders that Christ is risen!

- Let kids make Resurrection Rolls. Wrap a marshmallow in the center of a piece of Pillsbury Crescent dough, roll the dough in melted butter, sprinkle with cinnamon sugar, and bake according to package directions. Kids will be surprised when they break open the rolls and find them empty, like the tomb on Easter morning.

ALLERGY ALERT
See page 12.

▶ DIRECTIONS

Have kids form groups of four and give each team a Bible, paper, markers, and a copy of the scavenger list. On "go" have groups race to see who can complete the following tasks first:

1. Draw a picture of the animal in **Luke 22:60**.

2. Find something the color of the things people carried in **John 12:13**.

3. Find a small version or draw a picture of the item in **Mark 16:4**.

4. Draw a picture of the body part in **Luke 22:50**.

5. Make a paper version of what the soldiers made for Jesus in **John 19:2**.

6. Locate something the color of the robe in **Mark 15:17**.

7. Make a sign like the one in **Matthew 27:37**.

8. Tear out of paper a model of the item in **Mark 14:22**.

When groups are finished, have kids shout together, "Christ is risen!"

LISTEN CAREFULLY

Use this game to help kids learn how to listen to God.

WHAT YOU'LL NEED:

You'll need a blindfold.

FOR EXTRA IMPACT:

- Let each child have a turn being the listener and play the game again, but this time put on soft music in the background.

- Afterward, ask: How was this game like or unlike when we have distractions and can't hear God's voice? Explain. What are some distractions that keep us from hearing God's voice?

- Read aloud **Psalm 85:8** and challenge kids to spend some quiet time each day listening to God.

DIRECTIONS

Blindfold one person and have him or her face the group while standing about 20 feet away. Have a leader point to one of the other children. The child who's chosen attempts to move slowly and quietly toward the blindfolded person. The blindfolded player listens carefully for the approaching player and tries to point toward the location of the approaching player. The approaching player freezes once he or she has been located, and then another player is picked to move. The object is to get the kids close enough to the blindfolded player to tag him or her. Once the blindfolded person is tagged, blindfold another child.

Afterward ask: How easy or difficult was it to hear the approaching players? How is that similar to or different from listening to God?

MAKE 'EM SMILE

Kids learn about helping others.

WHAT YOU'LL NEED:

You'll need a piece of paper with a happy face on one side and a sad face on the other, neckties, purses or necklaces, and small toys.

FOR EXTRA IMPACT:

- Ask: Why should we help others? How does it feel to help others? Explain.

- Read aloud **Ecclesiastes 4:10**. Have kids each tell about a time a friend helped them.

- Let kids "finger-paint" smiling faces on waxed paper with chocolate pudding and then eat their tasty treats.

ALLERGY ALERT
See page 12.

DIRECTIONS

Form a circle. Have children each select a man's necktie, a woman's purse or necklace, or a small toy. You'll need one item for each child. Hold a piece of paper with a sad face on one side and a happy face on the other. Have children walk in a circle and sing these words to the tune of "Three Blind Mice":

I'll help you.
I'll help you.
Jesus wants me to.
Jesus wants me to.
I'll make you feel so very glad.
I'll make you feel so very glad.
'Cause I love you.
I love you.

After the song, hold the sad face over a child's head. If the child has a man's tie, ask: How can we help fathers feel happy when they're sad? If the child is holding a woman's item, ask: How can we help mothers feel happy? If the child is holding a toy, ask about brothers, sisters, or friends.

Then turn the paper to the happy face. Repeat until every child has had a turn.

MAKING SENSE

Kids learn about obedience to God.

WHAT YOU'LL NEED:

You'll need a bell, a picture, perfume, a stick of gum, a pencil, and a paper bag.

ALLERGY ALERT
See page 12.

FOR EXTRA IMPACT:

- Ask: Why does God want us to be obedient? How can we resist temptations?

- Read aloud **Matthew 26:41** and ask: Why do you think our spirits are willing but our bodies are weak? What does it mean to watch and pray?

DIRECTIONS

Place all the items in a paper bag. Ask kids to name their five senses (hearing, sight, smell, taste, touch). Tell them they'll be using some of their five senses today.

Have kids sit in a circle. Pass the bag around the circle. Have kids each reach into the bag but not look in it while trying to silently identify the five items. When children are sure they know what's in the bag, have them pass the bag to their left.

When the bag returns to you, see how many children correctly guessed the contents of the bag. Then ask: How did you use your senses to determine the contents? How easy or difficult was it to keep from using your sense of sight when it was your turn? How easy or difficult is it to obey all of your parents' or teachers' instructions?

Say: You might be tempted to think, "I know Mom said not to eat those cookies, but they smell so good." It's not always easy to obey because there are temptations all around us, but God wants us to be obedient.

LOW / MODERATE ENERGY

MATCHUP

This icebreaker works best with a large group.

WHAT YOU'LL NEED:

You'll need a copy of the questions and the body parts/characteristics list.

FOR EXTRA IMPACT:

- Read aloud **1 Corinthians 12:12,** and ask kids: Even though we are individual people, how do we form one body?

- Read aloud **1 Corinthians 12:27**. Ask: How are we the body of Christ? What part do you think you have in the body of Christ?

- Play the game again, but this time have kids join with everyone having the same characteristic. For example, everyone wearing shoes would touch elbows with another person. Once all kids are joined together, close in prayer, thanking God that we are one in Christ.

DIRECTIONS

Have kids stand up and move any chairs to the outside edges of your room. Tell kids that you'll call out characteristics and body parts. Then kids have to find someone with a matching characteristic and touch the body parts together that you called out. For example, if you call out "elbows and wearing the same color," kids must find someone wearing the same color and touch elbows with that person.

Call out these body parts and characteristics:

1. ears and the same kind of shoe

2. feet and the same grade

3. heads and a different grade

4. backs and the same length of hair

Each time kids match up, stop and discuss one of these questions: How long have you come to this church? Why do you come to this church? What is one way you know that God loves you? What is one prayer request you have?

Have pairs pray together before ending the game.

MIRROR ME

Kids learn the importance of being a good example to others.

WHAT YOU'LL NEED:

You'll need a Bible for each pair of kids.

FOR EXTRA IMPACT:

- Divide kids into five groups and give each group a different example (speech, life, love, faith, purity) from **1 Timothy 4:12**. Have groups write lists of behaviors for their examples. For speech, kids might write, "Say only kind words to others," or "Avoid gossip."

- Have groups share their lists with the class, then hang the lists on the wall.

- Have each child write one behavior for each example on the list. Challenge kids to apply those behaviors in their lives during the following week.

DIRECTIONS

Form pairs. Have kids in each pair choose who'll be the Example and who'll be the Follower. Have partners stand toe to toe, facing each other. Say: If you're the Example, it's your job to make motions and facial expressions for the Follower to follow. Remember, this isn't a competition, so you'll need to keep your motions slow and simple enough for your partner to follow. Followers, it's your job to mirror everything the Examples do.

Have kids play for a minute or two, then have them switch roles and play again.

Give each pair a Bible. Have kids read aloud **1 Timothy 4:11-12**. Then have all the kids form one circle. Ask: Was it easier to be the Example or the Follower in our activity? Why? Is it easier to be an Example or a Follower in real life? Explain. What did Paul tell Timothy about being a good example? How can you be a good example to your friends?

Say: Real friends are good examples for each other. Let's ask God to help us be good examples that our friends will want to follow.

Pray: Dear God, please help us be good examples for our friends. Thank you for sending Jesus as our perfect example. Amen.

MIXED EMOTIONS

Kids learn about the importance of following good leaders.

WHAT YOU'LL NEED:

You'll need a Bible.

FOR EXTRA IMPACT:

- Lead kids in a regular game of Follow the Leader, but turn out the lights so it's difficult to see. Afterward, ask: How was trying to follow the leader in this game like or unlike trying to follow the leader in the first game? Explain.

- Read aloud **John 8:12** and ask: What does it mean to you that Jesus is the light of the world? What does it mean that we will never walk in darkness if we follow Jesus?

DIRECTIONS

Have players form a circle, either standing or sitting. Choose one person to be a Volunteer and leave the room. Then choose a person in the room to be the Leader. The Leader performs a hand or body motion while the rest of the participants copy the Leader's movement without making it obvious that they're watching the Leader. After the group practices smoothly switching motions a few times, bring the Volunteer back into the room.

Ask the Volunteer to guess who's leading the group as the game is played. While trying not to be caught, the Leader should switch motions as the Volunteer looks around the circle. The idea is for all participants to quickly copy the Leader's new motions. Let the Volunteer have three guesses. Play until several children have had a turn to be a Volunteer or a Leader.

After the game is played, ask: How easy or difficult was it to identify the Leader? Why? How easy or difficult was it to follow the Leader? Explain. How easy or difficult is it to follow the right people at church or school? Explain.

Then read aloud **Mark 1:16-18** and ask: What does it mean to follow Christ?

MOLD IT

Kids love making Bible story creations.

WHAT YOU'LL NEED:

You'll need party packs of Play-Doh and paper strips with various Bible stories written on them.

FOR EXTRA IMPACT:

- After kids guess the Bible story, have older kids read aloud the Scripture passage. Tell younger kids a short paraphrase of the story.

- Have kids work together to make a clay diorama to display in the classroom. Let each child pick which part of the Bible story he or she wants to create in clay to add to the scene.

- Make a batch of edible modeling dough by mixing an 8-ounce package of cream cheese with ½ cup nonfat dry milk and 1 tablespoon honey. Let kids mold the dough to make edible story sculptures.

See page 12.

DIRECTIONS

Give each child Play-Doh and one Bible story strip. Tell children not to tell anyone their stories but to design something with their Play-Doh that could help others guess what their stories are. For example, if a child gets the story of the Tower of Babel, he or she could make a tower.

When kids finish their designs, have them guess what each one represents. Or have children form teams to guess the other team's design. This is a great review for all the Bible stories you've covered over a unit or the entire year.

LOW / MODERATE ENERGY

MUSICAL THANK-YOUS

This game helps kids thank God with a musical flair.

LOW / MODERATE ENERGY

WHAT YOU'LL NEED:

You'll need 1 chair for each child. For each chair, you'll need a different-color sheet of construction paper, cut in half. You'll also need tape and a music player.

FOR EXTRA IMPACT:

- Read aloud **Psalm 69:30,** and ask kids: Why should we give God thanks and praise? How do you think God feels when we thank him?

- Teach kids this rhyming prayer:

  *I thank you, God,
     for all you do.*

  *I praise your name
     and glorify you.*

- Instead of using chairs, play this game by having kids sit in a circle and pass different-colored plastic Easter eggs.

DIRECTIONS

Before class, place chairs back to back in a row, and tape half a sheet of construction paper to the back of each chair. Keep the other half sheet.

Play music, and have children walk around the chairs—just as in Musical Chairs. Stop the music, and have children find a seat. Choose a half sheet of paper. Whoever is seated in a chair with the matching color must stand and complete this sentence, "I thank God for…"

Continue, choosing a different color each time you stop the music to give children opportunities to come up with different reasons to thank God.

MYSTERY SOCK BOX

This fun game will keep kids guessing!

WHAT YOU'LL NEED:

You'll need an empty oatmeal box, tube sock, spoon, toy car, crayon, rock, and a pair of sunglasses.

FOR EXTRA IMPACT:

- Use themed items in your mystery box to go along with different Bible stories. For example, put a toy boat and small animal figurines in the box for a lesson on Noah.

- Let kids form pairs and take turns choosing different items from around the room to place inside a mystery paper bag. Have the partners take turns guessing the different items in the bag.

- Give kids each a lunch sack with a snack inside, such as cookies or crackers. Have kids guess what the snack is before they can eat it, then close in prayer thanking God for creating all things.

See page 12.

DIRECTIONS

Make a durable and unique mystery box for preschoolers. Secretly fill a large, empty oatmeal box with safe, familiar objects, such as a spoon, a toy car, a crayon, a rock, and a pair of sunglasses. Then carefully pull an old tube sock up and around the oatmeal box. The sock should fit snugly on the box.

Tell children that the box contains things God made. Then one at a time, have children put their hand through the sock and down into the box. Have children each feel an object and try to guess what it is.

After this guessing game, talk about whether God really made an object. Help children understand that even though God may not have made the exact object, he did create the elements that make the object. For example, God didn't make a toy car, but he did make the elements for the metal, rubber, and paint on the car.

Change the objects every now and then so kids can enjoy the mystery box over and over.

LOW / MODERATE ENERGY

ON THE ROAD TO DAMASCUS

This simple game will help kids get to know one another better.

WHAT YOU'LL NEED:

You'll need a Bible.

FOR EXTRA IMPACT:

- Ask: Why does God want us to be like Jesus? What are ways we can be more like Jesus?

- Give kids each a piece of clay, and have them mold an object that represents their talent or interest. Have an art show, and let kids display their works for each other to see. Ask: How can we use our talents to serve God?

▶ DIRECTIONS

Have kids form a circle. Read aloud **Acts 9:1-22**. Explain that just as Saul was on a journey, they, too, are on a journey to get to know Jesus. But before they leave, they'll need to pack their suitcases and get to know their traveling companions.

Have kids each think of an object that represents a talent or interest they have.

Say: We're on the road to Damascus. I'm [name], and I brought my [item of choice].

Have the person on your left repeat the phrase, your name and item, and add his or her own. With each turn, the list gets longer and kids must remember the names and interests of others.

Your list may sound something like this: "We're on the road to Damascus. Alice brought her Bible. Andy brought his baseball glove. Jan brought her math book. And I brought a paintbrush." If kids have trouble remembering, others can give hints.

The game is over when the last person has repeated everyone's name and object.

Say: God will make us more like Jesus and show us how to use our talents and interests to serve him on our journeys.

PASS THE PRAYER

Kids unwrap this lesson on prayer.

WHAT YOU'LL NEED:

You'll need a box, gift wrap, tape, paper, pen, and a music player.

FOR EXTRA IMPACT:

• Have kids form groups of four, and give each group a box with four prayers of thanksgiving written on four pieces of paper and wrapped in different layers around the box. Let each child have a turn unwrapping a layer. Then offer a prayer of thanksgiving.

• Give each child a small, plain white box. Have kids decorate the boxes with markers and then write their names on them, along with the words, "My Prayer Box."

• Have kids write prayer requests on slips of paper and put the requests in their prayer boxes. (Have younger kids draw pictures on slips of paper.) At the beginning of each class, have kids find partners, exchange their boxes, and pray for each other's requests.

DIRECTIONS

Wrap a box in several layers of wrapping paper. As you wrap, attach a prayer request to the top of each layer. Have a cassette or CD player handy to play upbeat music.

Have children sit in a circle. Turn on the music, and have kids pass the wrapped package around the circle.

Every now and then, stop the music. Whoever is holding the package when the music stops unwraps the first layer and reads the attached prayer request. You may need to read the requests for very early readers.

Start the music again. Continue playing until all the layers are unwrapped and every request is uncovered. The children can then either pray for all the requests with partners or in small groups.

LOW / MODERATE ENERGY

PAUL AND SILAS

Kids will love this new twist on "London Bridge."

WHAT YOU'LL NEED:

Nothing! This is a prop-free, prep-free game.

FOR EXTRA IMPACT:

- As you paraphrase the story of Paul and Silas in prison from **Acts 16:22-31**, let kids act it out. When you get to the earthquake, have kids roll around and yell, "Believe in Jesus and you will be saved." Ask: How do you think Paul and Silas felt when they were in prison? Explain. Why did they sing and praise God?

- Lead kids in singing their favorite praise song.

DIRECTIONS

Lead children in this variation of the "London Bridge" song and movements. Have two people form a bridge by holding hands. Then have other children line up and walk under the bridge as everyone sings these words.

First verse:

Paul and Silas preached the Word, preached the Word, preached the Word.

Paul and Silas preached the Word,

But they got thrown in jail. (Have the bridge lower and capture a child.)

Second verse:

Praising God will set them free, set them free, set them free. ("Rock" child back and forth in the lowered bridge.)

Praising God will set them free,

They got the victory! (Open bridge.)

Play until all children have a turn being "captured" in the bridge.

PICTURE RELAY

Kids draw the Easter story in this creative game.

WHAT YOU'LL NEED:

You'll need chalk and a chalkboard.

FOR EXTRA IMPACT:

- Let kids use colored chalk to draw their own renditions of the Easter story on construction paper. Spray the drawings with hair spray to seal the pictures.

- Display the pictures in the hall, and invite other classes to come see the artwork.

- Encourage kids to take their pictures home and use them to tell the Easter story to others.

DIRECTIONS

Form two teams. Have teams line up in front of a chalkboard. Give the first child in each line a piece of chalk. Tell teams that they're going to work together to draw a picture of Easter. Encourage kids to focus on the real Easter story about Jesus' death and resurrection.

On "go," each child should draw part of the picture and then pass the chalk to the child behind him or her. That child should draw another part, and so on. After the chalk returns to the first child in line, stop the game.

Ask each team to tell about its picture. Affirm both teams for their drawings. Then ask: How did you decide what to include in your picture? What are the most important elements of the Easter story?

LOW / MODERATE ENERGY

PRAYER IN MOTION

Kids will love this moving cheer to help them as they pray.

WHAT YOU'LL NEED:

Nothing! This is a prop-free, prep-free game.

FOR EXTRA IMPACT:

- Read aloud **James 5:13,** and ask kids: Why should we pray when we're in trouble? Why should we say prayers of praise and thanksgiving? How do you think God feels when we pray? How do you feel when you pray? Explain.

- Teach kids the words to this rhyme:

    *When I'm in trouble,
    I will pray*

    *And give God thanks and
    praise each day.*

DIRECTIONS

Number the four corners of your room. Have kids form a circle, and stand in the center of the circle. Ask kids to think about each statement you make and then move to the numbered corner that best fits their answer.

Say: Today I am most thankful for: my family (corner 1), my friends (corner 2), my home (corner 3), or my church (corner 4).

After kids move to their corners, say: Dear God, today we are thankful for (point to corner 1 and shout with the children "my family," point to corner 2 and shout with the children "my friends," point to corner 3 and shout with the children "my home," point to corner 4 and shout with the children "my church").

Repeat this process with different statements and numbered-corner answers.

PUZZLE PIECES

Kids will love this puzzling race.

WHAT YOU'LL NEED:

You'll need old Christmas cards, scissors, and drinking straws.

FOR EXTRA IMPACT:

- Have kids each glue a Christmas card picture onto a piece of paper and write the words to **Luke 2:10-11** on the back.

- Have kids each decorate an envelope, cut their card into puzzle pieces, and place the pieces in the envelope.

- Let kids find a partner, exchange envelopes, and then put the puzzles together. Kids can take their puzzles home as Christmas keepsakes or to give away.

DIRECTIONS

Form teams of four. Give each team a pair of scissors and the front of a Christmas card. Have each team cut its card into eight pieces. Then have teams mix up their puzzle pieces and lay them on a flat smooth surface. Give each child a drinking straw.

On "go," have kids suck on their straws to pick up a puzzle piece and move it to the proper puzzle position. After teams assemble their puzzles, have them exchange puzzles and play again.

LOW / MODERATE ENERGY

RAISE YOUR HANDS

Kids learn about the Israelites' victory over the Amalekites.

WHAT YOU'LL NEED:

You'll need a Bible, masking tape, and 5 Ping-Pong balls.

FOR EXTRA IMPACT:

- Read aloud **Psalm 140:6-7,** and ask: Why do you think God wants us to cry out to him when we face battles in life?

- Have kids make banners by decorating felt pennants with fabric scraps, ribbons, and buttons. Use paint pens to write, "The Lord is my banner." Encourage kids to hang the banners in their rooms as reminders to cry out to God when facing battles in life.

DIRECTIONS

Divide the room with a strip of masking tape on the floor. Place five Ping-Pong balls along the tape. Form two teams—the Israelites and the Amalekites.

Have teams stand on opposite sides of the tape. When you raise your hands into the air, the Israelites blow the balls toward one wall while the Amalekites stand still. When you lower your hands, the Amalekites blow toward the opposite wall, and the Israelites stand still. The first team to get two balls to the opposite wall wins. Hold your hands up longer for the Israelite team to win.

Read aloud **Exodus 17:8-16**. Ask: How did you feel as you played this game? Did you feel it was fair or unfair? Explain. What are some battles in your life that you need to win? How does God help you win battles?

SEARCHING FOR THE TRUTH

Kids learn how difficult it is sometimes to separate truth from fiction.

WHAT YOU'LL NEED:

You'll need a wading pool, ice cubes, and 20 to 30 clear marbles.

FOR EXTRA IMPACT:

- Read aloud **Hebrews 4:12,** and ask kids: What does it mean that God's Word is living and active? How does God's Word penetrate our hearts?

- Give each child a marble to take home as a reminder to cling to the truth of God's Word.

DIRECTIONS

Fill a wading pool with ice cubes, and place 20 to 30 clear marbles in the pool. Have kids take off their socks and shoes and then try to pick up the marbles with their toes.

After everyone has had a chance to try, ask: How easy or difficult was it to pick up the marbles with your toes? Explain. How were the marbles different from or similar to the ice? How is distinguishing between marbles and ice cubes with your toes like or unlike trying to decide what's true and what's not true?

Say: Sometimes it's hard to determine if something's true or false because what's false often looks or feels like truth. And just as our feet got cold and numb from the ice while we were looking for the marbles, sometimes false things can make us numb to the truth. The best way to know truth is to pick up and hold on to God's Word!

SHEPHERD, SHEPHERD

Kids will enjoy this fun twist on Hide and Seek.

WHAT YOU'LL NEED:

You'll need a small toy sheep.

FOR EXTRA IMPACT:

- Paraphrase the story of the lost sheep in **Luke 15:3-6,** and ask kids: How do you think the shepherd felt when he found his lost sheep? How was that like or unlike the way you felt in our game? Why does the shepherd look for his lost sheep?

- Read aloud **John 10:11,** and say: Jesus is the good shepherd, and we are his sheep. Because he loves us, he doesn't want us to be lost.

▶ DIRECTIONS

Have children sit in a circle, with one child seated in the center as the Shepherd. Place a small toy sheep on the floor behind the Shepherd. Have the Shepherd close his or her eyes. Silently point to one of the children seated in the circle. Have this child quietly sneak to the middle of the circle, take the toy sheep, and return to his or her place. Have all the children in the circle place their hands behind their backs. Then tell the Shepherd to open his or her eyes. Have children say:

Shepherd, shepherd, where's your sheep?
Someone took it while you were asleep!

The Shepherd then gets three guesses to find the sheep thief. If the guess is correct, the child with the sheep becomes the Shepherd. If, after three guesses, the Shepherd hasn't identified the correct sheep thief, reveal him or her and let this person become the Shepherd. Continue playing until each child has had a chance to be the Shepherd.

STICKS AND STONES

Kids will love this creative icebreaker.

WHAT YOU'LL NEED:

You'll need a stick (or toothpick), a small stone (or marble), and a feather for each child.

FOR EXTRA IMPACT:

- Have kids share with the class things that make them laugh. Then read aloud **Job 8:20-21,** and ask: Why does God fill us with laughter and joy? Explain.

- Have kids share with the class things that make them angry. Then read aloud **Ephesians 4:26.** Ask: How can we avoid sinning when we're angry?

- Have kids share with the class things that are difficult. Then read aloud **James 1:2-3.** Ask: How do difficulties or trials help our faith become strong?

DIRECTIONS

Place the sticks, stones, and feathers in the center of the room. Say: It's often hard to meet everyone and learn something about people in a group. This activity will help us have fun while learning more about each other. You'll each need a stick, a stone, and a feather to play this game. You'll also need to find a partner.

If there's an uneven number of children, make one group of three.

Say: Sit on the floor cross-legged, face your partner, and place the items in front of you. When I count to three, each of you will choose one item and place it between you and your partner. If your partner chooses a feather, you must tell one thing that tickles you or makes you laugh. If your partner chooses a stick, tell one thing that pokes at you or makes you angry. And if your partner chooses a stone, tell one thing that's hard for you to do.

Count to three, then allow time for partners to talk. Repeat the game several times. Then have kids find new partners.

When children have finished playing, let them take their feathers, sticks, and stones home as reminders of their new friends.

TEAM BINGO

Kids love this interactive Bingo game.

WHAT YOU'LL NEED:

You'll need copies of the Bingo questions.

FOR EXTRA IMPACT:

- Play a game of reverse Bingo by having kids fill the squares of a regular Bingo card with M&M's candies. As a number is called, kids get to eat the candy on that number.

- Have kids play games of Bingo, and give canned goods as prizes. Afterward, kids can box up the cans and donate them to a local charity.

ALLERGY ALERT
See page 12.

DIRECTIONS

Form teams of equal size. Then ask the questions in the list below. You may need to add more questions depending on children's responses. If children can answer yes to any question, have them stand up. Children can stand for only one question. When all the team members on a team are standing, the team yells, "Bingo!"

The questions:

Do you have a pet?

Do you have a barrette in your hair?

Are you wearing shoes without shoelaces?

Did you eat breakfast this morning?

Did you make your bed today?

THANKSGIVING BALLOON GAME

Kids give thanks with this fun game.

WHAT YOU'LL NEED:

You'll need balloons, newsprint, and a marker.

FOR EXTRA IMPACT:

- Have each group of four make a turkey from an inflated balloon (for the body), a construction-paper head, wiggly eyes, orange craft foam (for the waddle), construction paper feathers, and tape. Have kids write things they're thankful for on the feathers and tape them to the turkey's body.

- Let kids read what others are thankful for.

- Hang the turkeys from the ceiling as a festive classroom display.

DIRECTIONS

Have children make a list of things they're thankful for on a sheet of newsprint. When they're finished, have them take a good look at the list before you hide it.

Form a circle. Explain that children will use a balloon to help them give thanks to God. The balloon must not touch the floor. For a person to bat the balloon, he or she must say, "God, I thank you for..." and name one of the things from the list. Items can't be repeated. However, one person may be thankful for a family member such as "Dad," and another person may say "Dad" also because they're two different people.

As a variation, form several circles and see which circle can keep their thanksgiving and balloon going the longest. When a balloon touches the ground, that group must sit down.

TRUE SERVANTS

Kids learn the importance of serving others.

LOW / MODERATE ENERGY

WHAT YOU'LL NEED:

You'll need a Bible and various items, such as a pencil, sheet of paper, string, roll of tape, empty cup, towel, glass of water and piece of candy. You'll need one item for each child.

FOR EXTRA IMPACT:

- Using a deep basin of warm water and towels, let kids wash each other's feet.

- After the foot washing, ask: How was foot washing like or unlike the game we just played? How do you think the disciples felt having their feet washed by Jesus? Explain.

DIRECTIONS

Have children sit in a circle of chairs. In the middle of the circle, set out the different items for kids to see. One at a time, have kids each pick one item and use it in some way to serve someone else in the circle. Kids must pick an item that hasn't been used. Make sure everyone is served once.

Afterward, read aloud **John 13:3-5, 12-17**. Ask: How did you feel as you served other people? How did it feel to be served? Why did Jesus serve the disciples? How can we serve other people this week?

TRUST ME

Kids learn about trusting God.

WHAT YOU'LL NEED:

You'll need a Bible, cotton balls, spoons, bowls, and blindfolds.

FOR EXTRA IMPACT:

• Have kids form pairs and take a trust walk around the room with one child blindfolded and the other child leading the way. Have partners switch roles and play again.

• After the trust walk, ask kids: Was it easy or hard to trust your partner? How does that compare to trusting God? Explain.

• Let kids use the leftover cotton balls to decorate construction paper sheep. Attach the sheep to a bulletin board with the title, "Ewe can trust in God." Then have kids write on the board ways God provides for our needs.

DIRECTIONS

Form pairs. Lead pairs in the following activities. Have partners trade places for each event.

COTTON BALL CHASE—One partner blindfolds the other and guides the blindfolded partner in using a spoon to scoop up cotton balls and put them in a bowl.

BLIND FALL—One partner stands behind the other and catches the other partner as he or she falls back.

After kids play the games, ask: How did it feel to trust someone? How did it feel to be trusted? not trusted?

Read aloud **Genesis 22:1-19**. Ask: Why did Abraham trust God? How did God reward Abraham? Is it easy or difficult for you to trust God? Explain. What does this Scripture passage reveal about God that'll help you trust him?

TRY, TRY AGAIN

Kids learn about forgiveness.

WHAT YOU'LL NEED:

You'll need a Bible and masking tape.

FOR EXTRA IMPACT:

• Play the game again, giving each child another turn. This time have the spotters hold the players' arms to help them stay on the line. Ask: How can the second game remind you of the Scripture verse? What is grace? How is God's forgiveness of our sins a gift?

DIRECTIONS

Place a 10-foot strip of masking tape on the floor in the center of your room. Ask: Do any of you think you can walk along this line without stepping off?

As a child comes forward, say: Before you try to make it across, you need to spin around.

Provide spotters for this activity to keep line walkers safe. Carefully spin the first volunteer 10 times, and have him or her start at one end of the line and walk across to the other end.

After everyone has had a turn to walk the line, have kids sit in a circle. Ask: What did you think when I first asked if you could walk on the line? How did your thoughts change after you saw what you'd have to do?

Say: Sometimes we think we can "do" things to earn God's forgiveness. But the more we try, the more we fail.

Read **Ephesians 2:8-9**. Say: Our sins are forgiven only because of Jesus, not because of anything we can do.

TURKEY THANKS

Play Pin the Tail on the Turkey with your kids to celebrate all they're thankful for.

WHAT YOU'LL NEED:

You'll need poster board, tape, markers, construction paper, a blindfold, and turkey sandwiches.

FOR EXTRA IMPACT:

- Read aloud **1 Chronicles 29:13,** and ask kids: How do you think God feels when we give him thanks and praise?

- Afterward, put the turkey on a bulletin board, and have kids tape the feathers in the correct place. Write the words to **1 Chronicles 29:13** on the board.

- For a crafty snack, have kids spread a vanilla wafer with cream cheese, add raisin eyes, a candy corn nose, and a red gummy worm wattle.

See page 12.

DIRECTIONS

Before class, draw a large turkey without tail feathers on a sheet of poster board and tape it to the wall. Cut out turkey tail feathers to give to each child.

Have kids each draw a picture of something they're thankful for on their feather. Have kids show and explain their pictures. Line kids up in front of the turkey. Then blindfold children one at a time and turn them around three times. Have blindfolded kids tape their tail to the turkey.

Afterward, serve children turkey sandwiches and celebrate all that God has done for them.

LOW / MODERATE ENERGY

WHO AM I?

Kids will have a blast revealing new things about themselves and getting to know each other better.

WHAT YOU'LL NEED:

You'll need a photocopy for each child of the "Who Am I?" paper.

FOR EXTRA IMPACT:

- Read aloud **1 Corinthians 7:7**, and ask: Why do you think God gives each of us different gifts?

- Have kids tell what they think their gifts are and how they can use their gifts to serve God.

- Have kids each think of one specific act they can do with their gifts to serve God. Challenge kids to serve God during the week using their gifts and then report back to the class the next week.

DIRECTIONS

Before class, call each child and ask him or her to tell you something personal—but not embarrassing—that the other children may not know. Children may tell you that they've been to the Grand Canyon six times or that they can do a backward handspring. Tell kids not to tell anyone else in the class what they told you.

Then make a "Who Am I?" paper. Write what kids told you on the left-hand side of a sheet of paper, and write the children's names in mixed order on the right-hand side. Make enough photocopies for each child to have one.

Give a "Who Am I?" paper and a pencil to each child. Have kids draw lines to match names with the things kids have done, without giving away what they told you.

After everyone has had a chance to complete the "Who Am I?" paper, go through the list and have children reveal their personal items.

THE BEST OF
children's
ministry
MAGAZINE

GAMES FOR

HIGH ENERGY

A HELPING HAND

Kids learn to help others with this fun game of Tag.

WHAT YOU'LL NEED:

You'll need a Bible and blindfolds.

FOR EXTRA IMPACT:

- Challenge kids to each do one kind deed to help a friend during the week. Have kids report back next week.

- Have kids form groups of three and make a Helping Hands Snack. Kids can work together to put handfuls of mini-pretzels, M&M'S candies, and dried fruit into small plastic bags. Shake to mix, and enjoy!

ALLERGY ALERT
See page 12.

DIRECTIONS

Form pairs and give each pair a blindfold. Designate a base. Choose one pair to be "It". Have one partner of each pair put the blindfold over his or her eyes. Have partners hold hands and stand by the wall opposite the base. Have partners get to the base without being tagged by "It". If either partner is tagged, that pair is "It" also and tries to tag other pairs.

Play until everyone is either caught or on the base. Have partners switch roles and play again. Ask: How did you help your partner in this game? How do friends help each other?

Paraphrase **Philippians 2:19-23**. Then ask: What kinds of things do you do to help your friends? What kinds of things do you think Timothy did to help his friend Paul? How can you help a friend this week?

AVALANCHE

Kids practice teamwork in this challenging game.

WHAT YOU'LL NEED:

You'll need a Bible, newsprint, markers, and car tires.

FOR EXTRA IMPACT:

- Have kids form teams of four and plan a strategy to build a banana split. On "go," have teams race to see who can build it the fastest.

See page 12.

- Have kids vote on which team's banana split is the prettiest, tallest, and messiest. Then declare all the teams winners and have kids eat the treats.

- Afterward, ask: How did your team work together? How was this like or unlike working together in the Avalanche game?

DIRECTIONS

If you have a big class, form teams of 12 or more. If you have a smaller class, everyone is on the same team. Give each group a car tire. On "go," have each team try to get all its team members on its team's tire and stay there for five seconds. Don't let teams give up!

Afterward, give teams newsprint and a marker. Have teams each complete this sentence with as many phrases as possible and list the phrases on the newsprint: "In order to stop the avalanche of people falling off the tire, we had to…"

Some answers teams may arrive at include: "forget our initial awkwardness"; "get close to one another"; "believe it could be done"; "keep trying and not give up"; "get ideas from everyone"; "work together"; "keep making adjustments"; or "find the right balance."

Have teams each read their list. Then ask: How are the things on your lists like or unlike the things we have to do to be the kind of church God wants us to be? What happens to the church if someone refuses to do one of these things?

Read aloud **Romans 15:1-7**. Then close in prayer, asking God to help your group live out the verses in this passage.

BALLOON CRUNCH

This is a fun game that'll teach kids to work together.

WHAT YOU'LL NEED:

You'll need an inflated and tied-off balloon for each child. Attach a tag to each balloon, and write two body parts on each tag. For example, you might write, "head/elbow," "ear/ear," or "knee/hand."

FOR EXTRA IMPACT:

- Read aloud **1 Corinthians 12:12** and ask kids: How are we like many parts that form one body? What would have happened in our game if we hadn't worked together? What happens in life when we don't work together?

- Have kids list ways they can work together, such as helping a sick friend or helping with chores at home. Challenge kids to do one thing per day from the list during the week.

▶ DIRECTIONS

Have children stand in line, and give each child a body-parts balloon. Kids need to connect the body parts on their tags with the people next to them, keeping their balloons between those parts. Once your entire group is connected, have them bunch together like a giant organism while keeping their balloons in place.

Call out simple directions for the group, such as "walk across the room," "go up and then down these two stairs," or "turn around in a circle three times." As the organism moves, kids must keep their balloons in place. If a balloon falls, kids must follow the direction again.

After this game, ask: How easy or difficult was it for you to move together and keep your balloons from falling? What did you do to keep your balloons in place? Talk to children about what it means to be the body of Christ. Encourage children to consider the parallels between all the group parts working together in the game and the parts of the body of Christ working together.

BALLOON RELAY

Kids will love this fun relay.

WHAT YOU'LL NEED:

You'll need balloons.

FOR EXTRA IMPACT:

- Ask: Was it easy or difficult to keep the balloons in a line or control where they would land? Explain.

- Read aloud **Psalm 1:3-5**. Ask: How were the balloons in our game like or unlike the chaff that blows in the wind? What does it mean to be "planted by streams of water"? Why does God want us to bear fruit and prosper?

DIRECTIONS

Form teams of four to six. Have teams line up in rows at one end of the room. Designate a finish line 15 to 20 feet across the room.

Give each teammate a balloon. Have kids blow up their balloons but not tie them off. Have the first teammates in line aim their balloon at the finish line and let go of it. The balloon will fly through the air. Wherever the balloon lands, the person must go to that spot, blow up the balloon again, and let go of it. Have kids continue this process until they cross the finish line. Once a teammate crosses the finish line, the next teammate in line starts the process again.

BETHLEHEM OR BUST

Kids will enjoy this fun relay during the Christmas season.

WHAT YOU'LL NEED:

You'll need the following for each team: large jingle bell, stick horse or mop, broom, and laundry basket.

FOR EXTRA IMPACT:

• Have kids use frosting and candies to decorate angel-shaped sugar cookies.

• As kids eat their angel cookies, read aloud **Luke 2:1-20**.

• Have kids each make a barefoot footprint with white paint on blue construction paper for an angel's body, then add white handprints for the wings. Kids can add a decorated construction paper head and halo and then write, "Glory to God in the highest!" across the top of the page.

▶ DIRECTIONS

Form teams of six or fewer, and have the teams line up at one end of the room with the props at the other end. Give the first person in each line a jingle bell to shake as he or she runs to the other end of the room and performs a series of activities. Once kids have completed all the activities, have them shake the bells as they return to their teams and pass the bells to the next people in line. Play until everyone has had a chance to do the activities.

The activities:

DONKEY RIDE—Ride a stick horse or mop in a circle and say, "Giddyup, giddyup." Lay down the "horse."

THE INN—Wave a broom in the air, and say, "No 'broom' in the inn."

MANGER—Sit in a laundry basket and say, "They laid him in a manger."

ANGEL—Flap your arms like wings and say, "Glory in the highest."

BIG FISH, LITTLE FISH

Kids can play this variation of Tag when your lesson is about fish or fishermen.

You'll need jump-ropes.

FOR EXTRA IMPACT:

- Read aloud **Matthew 4:18-20**, and ask kids: What do you think it means to fish for men? What does it mean to follow Jesus? Why does he want us to follow him?

- Fill a child's wading pool with water and plastic fish. Let kids "fish" with a net. For every fish they catch, they can say one way to serve Jesus.

DIRECTIONS

Use jump-ropes to form two circular "fish nets" on the floor on opposite sides of the room.

Choose two children to be fishermen, and say: Jesus had many friends who were fishermen. They caught lots of fish, and then they sold the fish in the market for people to eat. Let's play a game about fish. When I call out, "Big fish, little fish, swim, swim, swim!" everyone will run from the fishermen. If a fisherman tags you, go stand inside one of the fish nets. When the nets get too crowded, I'll call out, "Big fish, little fish, swim away free!" Then you can all escape and play again.

Play for several minutes. Change fishermen often.

BIGGER AND BETTER SCAVENGER HUNT

Kids will enjoy this fun new twist on an old favorite.

WHAT YOU'LL NEED:

You'll need a penny for each child and an adult driver for each group of children. For the banana splits, you'll need clean, new PVC rain gutters; ice cream; bananas; toppings; and spoons.

ALLERGY ALERT

See page 12.

FOR EXTRA IMPACT:

- As kids eat their banana splits, read aloud **Ecclesiastes 2:13**. Ask kids: Why is wisdom better than foolishness? light better than darkness? How is that like or unlike exchanging items for better things on our scavenger hunt?

- Have kids think of things they can do better, such as work harder in school or help around the house more. Challenge kids to pick one thing they'd like to do better and work at it the following week.

DIRECTIONS

Form groups of six children and one adult driver. Give each child a penny. For two hours, group members must each go to a different house, tell what church they're from, and explain the Bigger and Better scavenger hunt. Kids might say, "I have a penny. Can you give me something bigger and better than a penny?" Kids should exchange eight times at different houses.

While kids are gone, adult volunteers wash and attach 10 feet of plastic PVC rain gutters from the hardware store. Then adults make a great banana-split boat by placing one long row of pipe on pushed-together tables. (You can adjust the size of this boat depending on the number of kids. About 6 inches per child is enough.)

When kids return, an independent panel of judges chooses the winning Bigger and Better item. Then kids use tons of ice cream, bananas, and toppings to make a giant banana split.

While they eat, kids can tell their stories and laugh about all that happened.

BURDENS

Kids bear each other's "burdens" in this relay race.

WHAT YOU'LL NEED:

You'll need a Bible and blankets.

FOR EXTRA IMPACT:

- Have kids play again, but this time have only one person sit on the blanket and have the three team members pull the blanket. Ask kids: Which game was easier? Why? How is that like or unlike working together to help each other bear burdens?

- Serve kids "Burden-less" Buns for snack. As kids eat honey buns, read aloud **Psalm 68:19**. Have kids close in prayer and thank God for being our burden-bearer.

ALLERGY ALERT
See page 12.

DIRECTIONS

Form teams of no more than four. Give each team a blanket. Have teams each line up at one end of the room.

One team member sits on the blanket, and another teammate pulls him or her to the other end of the room.

The "pulling" team member gets on the blanket with the first child and another child pulls both teammates to the other end of the room.

The "pulling" team member gets on the blanket with the first two children and another child pulls all three teammates to the other end of the room.

If a child can't pull his or her teammates, have one or more kids from the blanket get up to help.

After the game, ask: How easy or difficult was this game? Explain.

Read aloud **Galatians 6:2**. Ask: What is a *burden*? How do you "bear" a burden? Ask children if they have any burdens they'd like the other children to pray for. Then pray for the needs children mention.

CATCH THE GOSSIP

Kids learn how quickly gossip can get out of hand.

WHAT YOU'LL NEED:

You'll need a Bible, masking tape, 2 rotating fans, and a bag of shredded paper.

FOR EXTRA IMPACT:

• Have kids make Gossip Gobblers for a snack. Melt together 3 tablespoons butter and 1 package of marshmallows. Mix in 6 cups of chow mein noodles. Form into balls, and place on wax paper to cool.

• As kids eat the tasty treats, ask: Have you ever been gossiped about? How did that feel?

ALLERGY ALERT
See page 12.

DIRECTIONS

Before class, use masking tape to form a circle on the floor. The circle should be large enough for all the children to fit inside it. Put two rotating fans in different corners of the room, facing the circle.

Show the children a bag of shredded paper. Say: Let's pretend this shredded paper is gossip. Ask: Who can tell me examples of gossip?

Say: When the wind blows, try to capture this gossip to keep it from spreading, but don't step out of the circle.

Turn on the first fan. Sprinkle the paper in front of the fan. Repeat this action until both fans are on. Continue the game until children tire of it.

Afterward, read aloud **Proverbs 11:13** and **20:19**. Ask: How easy was it to capture this gossip and stay inside the circle? How easy or difficult is it to capture real gossip? Were you able to capture all this gossip? Why or why not? How is this game like or unlike what happens with real gossip? According to these verses, how does God feel about gossip? What can we do instead of gossiping about people when we know a secret?

CHAIN-GANG RELAY

Use this cooperative relay to help your kids build teamwork and coordination.

WHAT YOU'LL NEED:

You'll need a Bible; crepe-paper streamer rolls; and obstacle course items from your classroom, such as chairs and trash cans.

FOR EXTRA IMPACT:

- Have kids make paper chains out of construction paper strips. Each child needs a chain long enough to fit around his or her ankle.

- Have kids tape the chains around their ankles. Play praise music, and let kids sing along. When you stop the music, have kids jump up, break their ankle chains, and shout, "God sets us free!"

DIRECTIONS

Beforehand, set up an obstacle course using classroom items such as chairs, trash cans, and other items kids will have to maneuver around.

Form relay lines. Give the first person in each line a crepe-paper streamer roll. Have the kids on each team tie themselves together by their left ankles. Say: On "go," your team must run through the obstacle course together without breaking your bond. That means you'll have to work together. If you break the streamer, you must go back to the starting line, tie yourselves together again, and start over.

Once the race is over, ask: What was difficult about the race? Were you able to work together? Why or why not? What made it easier to maneuver the obstacle course? What made it more difficult?

Read aloud **Acts 16:16-31**. Ask: How do you think Paul and Silas felt when they were forced into the jail? How do you think their bond with God helped them? How is that like or unlike the bond you experienced today?

CHAIR SHARE

Kids love this wacky game of sharing.

WHAT YOU'LL NEED:

You'll need 1 chair for every 2 children.

FOR EXTRA IMPACT:

- Read aloud **Hebrews 13:16,** and ask kids: Why does sharing with others please God? What would've happened in our game if we hadn't shared with each other? How is sharing a sacrifice? What sacrifice did Jesus make for us?

- Have kids tell ways they can share with others. Challenge kids to sacrifice and share one thing each day with someone they know.

▶ DIRECTIONS

Form a circle with the chairs. Have children sit on the chairs. They'll have to share. Call out the following statements, and have children move appropriately. Children must be sitting on a chair or on the lap of someone who's on a chair. After each statement, give children time to discuss their answers. Then take away a chair.

The statements (use the items in parentheses for more statements):

- If you have a pet (bicycle, Rollerblades, brother), move two chairs to your left.

- If you were born in the summer (winter, fall, spring), move three chairs to your right.

- If you like ice cream (pizza, spinach, hot dogs), move one chair to your right.

- If you enjoy swimming (baseball, Bingo, video games), move five chairs to your left.

CHORES RELAY

Kids work together in this fun relay.

WHAT YOU'LL NEED:

You'll need bread, plastic knives, cream cheese, jelly, potatoes, brooms, large plastic garbage bags with twist ties, newspaper, balloons, and tape.

See page 12.

FOR EXTRA IMPACT:

• Have kids each write a list of the chores they have to do at home. If any kids don't have assigned chores, have them write things they can do at home to help out.

• Form pairs and let partners share their lists. Ask: Why is it important to help out around the house?

• Read aloud **Deuteronomy 10:12-13,** and ask: How are we serving God when do chores?

DIRECTIONS

Have kids form teams of four. Start teams one at a time at Station 1.

Station 1: **SNACK BREAK**—Have each person slice a piece of bread in half, spread with cream cheese and jelly, put the halves together, and eat the sandwich. It must be swallowed before going to Station 2.

Station 2: **CARRYING GROCERIES**—Have each team member put a potato on each foot and shuffle to Station 3. If a potato rolls off, the child must stop and replace it before going on.

Station 3: **TRASH DETAIL**—Set up an obstacle course by taping five balloons to the floor about 3 feet apart in a straight line. Stuff a large plastic garbage bag with newspaper, and secure it with a twist-tie. Have each team member take a turn using a broom to move the "garbage" around the balloons.

When all teams have completed the course, ask: How did it feel to tackle each chore all by yourself? Would it have been easier if your team worked together in each station? What are some ways you can work together with your family members to make chore time easier at home?

CREATION RACE

Kids get creative in this fun relay race.

WHAT YOU'LL NEED:

You'll need a photocopy of the instructions for each team.

FOR EXTRA IMPACT:

- Ask kids: How easy or difficult was it to be creative and find the props you needed for the game? Explain. Why did God make us creative?

- Read aloud **Genesis 1:27,** and ask kids: What does it mean to be created in God's image?

- Have kids make a creation crunch snack by mixing Goldfish crackers and M&M's candies. As they eat the treat, read aloud **Genesis 1–2:2**.

See page 12.

DIRECTIONS

Form two teams and designate a goal line. Give each team a photocopy of the following instructions. Explain that a different person in each team should perform each step. Encourage kids to be creative in finding props, such as use a hat pulled over the eyes for the blindfold.

The steps:

1. Lead a blindfolded person to the goal line to represent night. At the goal line, have the person remove his or her blindfold to represent day and return to your starting place.

2. Carry a small container of water to the goal line, drink it, and run back to represent water and sky.

3. Carry a handful of dirt to the goal line to represent the earth. Make a small hill with it and then return.

4. Carry a small stick to the goal line. Draw a sun, moon, and star in the dirt to represent the lights.

5. With two pieces of paper, make a bird to represent flying creatures. Carry the bird to the goal line, leave it, and return.

6. Using small sticks, make a human figure to represent humankind. Carry the figure to the goal line, leave it, and return.

7. All teammates run to the goal line and sit in a circle.

DODGE THE STONES

Play this game to help kids re-create the battle between David and Goliath.

WHAT YOU'LL NEED:

You'll need various large obstacle items, such as plastic garbage cans, tables, and chairs; boundary markers, such as orange cones; buckets; large sponges; water; and towels.

FOR EXTRA IMPACT:

• Give kids rock candy for a snack. As they eat the treat, paraphrase the story of David and Goliath from **1 Samuel 17**.

ALLERGY ALERT
See page 12.

• Read aloud **Psalm 46:1,** and ask: How does God give us strength the way he gave David strength?

• Have kids find partners and share ways God has helped them in times of trouble. Close in prayer, thanking God that he is our refuge and strength.

DIRECTIONS

Create an outdoor play area using boundary markers. Place large obstacles kids can hide behind within the boundaries.

Choose several kids to be "stone throwers," and station them just outside the boundaries. Give the stone throwers buckets of water and sponges. Tell the other kids that the object of the game is to run from one end of the play area to the other without being "stoned" by wet sponges.

Play several times, and have kids switch roles so everyone has a chance to cool off by getting "stoned" with the wet sponges.

DRY-OFF DEBRIEF: Ask: How did it feel to throw "stones" at kids? What helped you dodge the stones? How do you think David felt when he stoned Goliath? What are some "Goliaths" that you have to defeat daily? How does God help us in these situations?

EYE OF THE NEEDLE

Kids learn what it takes to get to heaven.

WHAT YOU'LL NEED:

You'll need 2 large cardboard boxes, 2 Hula-Hoops, and 2 small cardboard crosses.

FOR EXTRA IMPACT:

- Have kids find partners and cut out pictures from old magazines of things that can keep us from Jesus. Let kids glue the pictures onto construction paper to create collages.

- Have pairs take turns telling the group about their pictures, then put the collages on a bulletin board. At the top of the board, write, "To Jesus I will cling, not to toys or money or things."

- Give each child a cardboard cross to decorate with craft materials. Then let kids take their crosses home as reminders that Jesus is the only way to heaven.

▶ DIRECTIONS

Before class, cut a hole in each box large enough for a child to fit through, but smaller than a Hula-Hoop.

Form two teams, and have each team line up opposite its box. Give the first child in each line a Hula-Hoop. Say: This hoop represents all your toys, money, and riches. Run to your team's box, crawl through the hole to "heaven" with your hoop, then run back, and give the hoop to the next person on your team.

Begin the race. It won't take children long to see that the hoop won't fit through the hole. After several minutes, stop the game and have kids line up to start over.

Give each line leader a cardboard cross instead of a hoop. Say: This cross represents Jesus.

Have kids run the relay again. This time they'll be able to get through the hole easily.

After the race, ask: Which item was easier to race with? Explain. How can toys, money, or riches slow us down or keep us away from Jesus? What do we need to do to get to heaven?

Read aloud **Matthew 19:23-26**, and discuss how the game illustrates the passage.

FIND YOUR FAMILY

This game will help children get to know other class members.

WHAT YOU'LL NEED:

You'll need a pen and slips of paper.

FOR EXTRA IMPACT:

- Read aloud **Galatians 6:9-10,** and ask kids: Who belongs to the family of believers? Why should we "do good to all people"?

- Have family groups make lists of good things we can do for others and then share their lists with the class.

DIRECTIONS

Think of animal families, each with a dad, mom, sister, and baby. Then write one family member on each slip of paper. For example, one family might be Dad Chicken, Mom Chicken, Sister Chicken, and Baby Chicken. Use a different animal for each family. Give each player one folded slip of paper. On "go," kids should walk around trading papers with everyone else in the room, trying to make as many exchanges as possible. They should not look at the papers.

After two minutes, call out, "Find your family." Kids should then look at their papers and, without speaking, find their family members by acting out the animals on their papers. When players find their families, they must sit in order from Dad to Baby in a line on the floor. Then have family members tell their real names to one another and a fun tidbit about themselves, such as their favorite ice cream or animal.

FOLLOW ME

Lead kids in this fun game to learn more about God.

WHAT YOU'LL NEED:

You'll need a flashlight and ties or scarves.

FOR EXTRA IMPACT:

- Read aloud **1 John 1:5,** and ask: What do you think it means that God is light? How can we be God's light to others?
- Teach kids the words to this rhyme:

  The Bible says that God is light.

  He will guide me day and night.

▶ DIRECTIONS

Say: The Bible says that God is light. And God wants us to follow him.

Form pairs. Help partners tie their legs so the duo becomes three-legged. Then make the room dark, and have each pair chase the light of a flashlight as you shine it.

After playing this game for a while, have children sit in a circle. Ask: How did you help each other follow the light? How can you help each other follow God?

Say: We can help each other follow God by praying for each other and by coming to church together. Let's pray and ask God to help us follow him.

Close in prayer.

FOLLOWING JESUS

Teach children about following Jesus with a fun game about following.

WHAT YOU'LL NEED:

You'll need a large stuffed animal, adhesive bandages, a bucket, blocks, a bowl, animal crackers, and paper cups.

FOR EXTRA IMPACT:

- Tell kids you're going to play another game of Follow the Leader. Turn off the lights and lead kids around a safe path in your room. Ask: Was it easy or hard to follow the leader in the dark? Explain.

- Read aloud **John 8:12**.

- Give kids small flashlights, and lead them around the room again. Say: Jesus tells us he is the light of the world and as long as we follow him, we will have his light.

DIRECTIONS

Before children arrive, set up the following stations. Then have children do the actions.

Place a large stuffed animal on a table along with a bandage (with wrapper removed) for each child. Say: Jesus healed the sick. We can help people who are sick, too. Have each child place a bandage on the animal.

Place a bucket and a pile of blocks on the floor. Say: Just as Jesus was helpful to others, we can be helpful too. Have each child pick up a block to "put away" in the bucket.

Say: We can be kind and loving to each other, just as Jesus was. Have children give each other hugs.

Place a bowl of animal crackers and a paper cup for each child on a table. Say: Jesus fed many people. We can feed others, too. Have children feed each other by filling cups with crackers and giving them to one another.

Close with the following prayer: Thank you, Jesus, for being our leader and showing us how to live. Help us follow you day by day, doing the same things you did for others. Amen.

FOOT RELAY

Build group unity with this game.

WHAT YOU'LL NEED:

You'll need small classroom items.

FOR EXTRA IMPACT:

- Have kids form teams. Let teams race to see who can complete the relay first. Ask: What would've happened in our game if team members hadn't worked together to move the items down the line? Explain.

- Read aloud **Psalm 133:1**, and ask: How is our game like or unlike living in unity as the verse says? Explain.

► DIRECTIONS

Make sure all kids are wearing pants or shorts for this game. Have each child find one item in your room. Kids may have duplicate items. The item can't be breakable, can't have sharp edges (such as scissors or a pencil), and can't be bigger than a loaf of bread.

Have children place their items in a pile at one end of the room and line up behind the pile. Then have kids lie on the floor with their knees bent and one foot beside each side of the child's head in front of them. It's OK if the line curves around the room.

On "go," have the first child in line place an item between his or her feet and pass it overhead to the next child. That child must grasp the item between his or her feet and pass it to the next child. No hands!

Time the children. After they have passed all the items to the end, celebrate kids' teamwork. Then play again, and try to beat the kids' first time.

FRUIT OF THE SPIRIT SCRAMBLE

Kids learn about the fruit of the Spirit with this action-packed game.

WHAT YOU'LL NEED:

You'll need an index card for each child, a Bible, a pen, and chairs. You'll need 1 less chair than the number of participants.

FOR EXTRA IMPACT:

- Give each child a set of the fruit of the Spirit cards. As you read **Galatians 5:22-23**, have kids jump up, wave the card with that fruit of the Spirit on it, and call out the name of the fruit.

- Have kids find partners, put together their fruit of the Spirit cards, and play a game of Memory.

- Have kids make a fruit basket bonanza for snack by filling sponge-cake cups with different types of fresh fruit slices.

See page 12.

▶ DIRECTIONS

Write the nine fruits of the spirit on separate index cards. Make sure there are enough cards for each child to have one card. If you have fewer than nine children, give some children more than one card. Add a symbol to each card to help nonreaders—a heart for love or a balloon for joy, for example.

Have kids sit in a circle of chairs that has one less chair than the number of participants. Give each child a card, quietly whispering the words to those who can't read.

The child without a chair stands in the middle and calls out one of the fruits of the spirit. Each child holding that fruit must vacate his or her chair and find another chair. The child in the middle must also find a chair. The child left without a chair stands in the middle and calls out the next fruit.

Every now and then, the caller may call out, "Walk in the spirit!" Then all the children should quickly find new chairs. The child left standing calls out the next fruit.

When the game is over, collect the cards to use again. Then read **Galatians 5:22-26** aloud, and discuss the fruits of the Spirit.

GO, TEAM!

This game emphasizes cooperation and problem solving.

WHAT YOU'LL NEED:

You'll need 2 soft foam balls.

FOR EXTRA IMPACT:

- Ask: How easy was it to follow the directions in our game? Explain. How easy is to follow Jesus? Explain.

- Read **Matthew 16:24-25** aloud, and ask: What does it mean to take up your cross and follow Jesus? Why does Jesus want us to follow him?

- Have kids work together and write a list of ways we can follow Jesus. Hang the list on the wall as a reminder to kids.

DIRECTIONS

Form two teams. Have team members number off from one to three. Explain that ones can pick up things, twos can throw things, and threes can hand off things.

Point out the boundaries of your playing area. Explain to kids that the goal of this game is to tag every player on the opposing team and put them out. Place two soft balls in the center of the teams, and yell "go."

Kids may be tagged by being hit or touched by a ball below the waist. Remind kids to remember their special skills and to work together.

For added fun in the warm summer months, use two buckets of water and large sponges for this game.

GOOD SAMARITAN GAME

Kids learn how Jesus wants us to take care of each other.

WHAT YOU'LL NEED:

You'll need a Bible, adhesive bandages, and cups of water.

FOR EXTRA IMPACT:

- Read aloud **Romans 15:1-2**, and ask kids: Why are we to help those who are weaker than ourselves? If you saw another child at school being picked on or teased, how would you respond according to this passage?

- Have kids each stick bandages onto an index card to form a cross, and then write, "'Love your neighbor as yourself'—Luke 10:27" on the cards.

DIRECTIONS

Form teams of four. Choose one person from each team to be the hurt man who was robbed and beaten on his way to Jericho. Have the hurt people lie on the floor at the end of the room opposite their teams. Give each team a supply of 10 to 15 adhesive bandages and a cup of water.

On "go," teams race with their supplies to their hurt team members. The goal is to put 10 bandages on the hurt neighbor, give him or her a drink of water, and carry the person back to the starting point.

Once every team has accomplished this, read aloud **Luke 10:25-37**. Ask: How did you feel when you were helping the hurt person? If you were the hurt person, how did you feel while you were being helped? How would you feel if you were hurt like the man in the parable and no one stopped to help you? What do you think Jesus meant when he said, "Love your neighbor as yourself"? What can you do to help others in need?

HANDY FOOTRACE

Kids will love this goofy footrace.

WHAT YOU'LL NEED:

You'll need masking tape, construction paper, safety scissors, and markers.

FOR EXTRA IMPACT:

- Read aloud **Isaiah 52:7,** and ask kids: What do you think this verse means? How can we bring the good news of Jesus to others?

- Challenge kids to tell others about Jesus.

- Have kids trace their footprints on construction paper, cut them out, glue them to a contrasting color of construction paper, and write at the top of the paper, "My feet bring the good news of Jesus."

▶ DIRECTIONS

Using masking tape, create a starting line on the floor or ground and a finish line 30 feet away. Place supplies of construction paper, markers, safety scissors, and 12-inch strips of masking tape at each line.

As kids arrive, have them form pairs. On "go," have one child trace his or her feet on construction paper and then cut them out. Using masking tape, have kids affix their cutout feet to their hands. The person with new "feet" will put his or her palms on the ground while the partner picks up his or her legs wheelbarrow-style. The pair then scrambles to the finish line, but if they lose a foot along the way, they must stop and reattach it. Once the team crosses the finish line, partners switch roles, make new feet, and head the other direction to cross the start line.

HARVEST RELAY

Use this fun game to teach kids about God's harvest.

WHAT YOU'LL NEED:

You'll need a Bible, large tub, water, cranberries, apples, containers, plastic spoons, and a scale.

ALLERGY ALERT
See page 12.

FOR EXTRA IMPACT:

• Ask: Have you ever felt like giving up on something? What happened?

• Read aloud **Galatians 6:9,** and ask: How can this verse encourage you when you feel like giving up?

• Cut the uneaten apples in half. Have kids each apply paint to an apple half and press the apple all over a sheet of paper to make apple prints. Then have them write, "Don't grow weary… reap a harvest for God."

DIRECTIONS

At one end of the room, fill a large tub with cold water, cranberries, and a few apples. At the other end of the room, form teams of four or five. Give each child a plastic spoon and each team the same size container. Each team has five minutes to make its container the heaviest. You'll need a scale at the end of the game.

On "go," one child from each team runs to the tub, scoops up cranberries or apples using only a plastic spoon (no hands), and returns to dump cranberries or apples into the team's container. If the child drops the fruit on the way back, he or she has to pick it up with the spoon. The next person in line repeats the process.

Weigh the containers at the end of the relay. As kids are enjoying the fruit, ask: How easy or difficult was it to get the cranberries in the bucket? How about the apples?

Read aloud **Luke 10:2.** Say: God wants us to help others know him. Sometimes it's easy to tell others about God, just as it was easy to pick up the cranberries. Sometimes it's harder, like picking up the apples. But God wants us to keep trying!

HUG TAG

This game of hugs will bring laughter and joy to your kids.

WHAT YOU'LL NEED:

You'll need hats for every 10 children.

FOR EXTRA IMPACT:

- Read aloud **1 John 4:11,** and ask kids:

- Besides giving hugs, what are other ways we can show love to our friends?

- Teach kids the words to this rhyme:

    Love your friends as God loves you,

    Show your love in all you do.

- Have kids each place several Hershey's Hugs and Kisses chocolates in a square of tissue paper and tie with a ribbon. Attach cards preprinted with the words of **1 John 4:11** to the bundles. Encourage kids to give the bundles to their friends.

See page 12.

DIRECTIONS

Choose a Tagger for every 10 children. Give each Tagger a hat. Tell children that the only way they can be safe from the Tagger is if they're hugging someone. Kids can form hugging groups of any number. On a signal, all kids must run and try to find new hugging groups. If anyone is tagged while "unhugged," that person becomes the Tagger and wears the tagging hat.

HUMAN JACKS

Kids will have a ball with this fun game.

WHAT YOU'LL NEED:

You'll need a playground ball.

FOR EXTRA IMPACT:

- Read aloud **Colossians 3:13-14,** and ask kids: Why does God want us to forgive others when they hurt us? Why does God forgive our sins? What would've happened in our game if we hadn't been willing to come together when "twosies" and "threesies" were called? How is that like or unlike what happens when we don't forgive each other?

- Have kids form pairs and play an actual game of Jacks. After kids call out "onesies" and pick up their jacks, have them each share one way to show love to others. After "twosies" are called, tell two ways to show love and so on.

DIRECTIONS

Form a circle. Choose one child to be the Tosser and hand him or her a playground ball.

Say: This game is played like Jacks, only we're using people instead of jacks. The Tosser will toss the ball high in the air and begin to call out "onesies." You must form groups of one before the Tosser catches the ball. Then the Tosser will toss the ball again and say "twosies." Run to form groups of two before he or she catches the ball. If you can't find a group before the Tosser catches the ball, sit down until he or she calls the next group number. We'll continue until everyone forms one large group.

Continue playing until each child has been the Tosser.

IT'S EASTER

Kids will love this "egg-citing" game.

WHAT YOU'LL NEED:

You'll need a praise music CD, a CD player, a plastic Easter egg for each child, and a slip of paper with "It's Easter!" written on it. Put the paper inside one of the eggs.

FOR EXTRA IMPACT:

- Have kids each fill their plastic eggs with beans, tightly close the eggs, and tape them shut. Play praise music, and have kids shake their eggs along with the music.

- Hide a chocolate Easter egg for each child, and let kids have an Easter egg hunt.

- Let kids eat their chocolate treats and ask: What are some ways your family celebrates Easter? What does Easter mean to you?

See page 12.

▶ DIRECTIONS

Form a circle. Give each child a plastic egg. Designate a corner of the room as "base." Play music and have children pass the eggs to their left so they're always holding an egg.

When the music stops, have children open their eggs. The child with the "It's Easter!" slip is "It" and must shout, "It's Easter!" All the children run from "It" to get to the designated base before "It" tags them. Anyone who's tagged stands in the center of the circle for the next round of the game.

Put the slip in a plastic egg, mix up the eggs, and pass them out. Play again, allowing the children in the center of the circle to run from "It" when "It's Easter!" is called out. If they aren't tagged, they can get out of the center of the circle. Play until children tire of this game.

JESUS LOVES YOU

Kids will love this new twist on an old favorite.

WHAT YOU'LL NEED:

You'll need a Bible.

FOR EXTRA IMPACT:

• Ask: How can we show others that we love them?

• Have kids form pairs and each create their partner's portrait by frosting cookies and using candies to create faces. Then have partners trade portraits and eat their yummy masterpieces.

ALLERGY ALERT
See page 12.

• Close by leading kids in singing a round of "Jesus Loves Me."

DIRECTIONS

Play the familiar game of Duck, Duck, Goose, but instead of saying "duck, duck, goose," have the child who is "It" say, "Jesus loves, loves, loves YOU!"

Have children sit in a circle. The child who is "It" walks around the circle and pats each child's head while saying only one word in the phrase. When the child says "you," the child whose head is tapped jumps up and chases "It" back to the tagged child's space.

If the tagged child catches "It," the child who's "It" must sit in the middle of the circle until someone replaces him or her. The new child is "It" and continues the game. Remind children to make sure everyone gets a turn because Jesus loves everyone in the circle.

Afterward, read aloud **1 John 4:9-10** in an easy-to-understand translation.

JUGGLING RACE

Kids learn how difficult it can be to juggle many things.

WHAT YOU'LL NEED:

You'll need 2 marbles, 2 golf balls, 2 basketballs, 2 soccer balls, 2 footballs, and 2 baseballs.

FOR EXTRA IMPACT:

- Give kids each one inflated balloon with "Jesus" written on it, and have kids bat the balloons in the air. Afterward ask: Was it easier trying to run while juggling all the balls or batting only one balloon in the air? Explain.

- Let kids try to bat the balloon again, but this time tell them to keep their eyes closed. Read aloud **Hebrews 12:2,** and ask: What happens in real life if we take our eyes off of Jesus?

- Let kids keep the balloons. Remind them to keep their eyes on Jesus.

DIRECTIONS

Form two teams. Have teams line up at one end of the room. Place all the balls except the marbles at the other end of the room. For younger kids, use no more than three balls for each team. Hand a marble to the first person in line on each team.

On "go," have the first person in each team run to the other end of the room, pick up another ball, return, and hand off the balls to the next person. The next person runs with two balls and picks up a third ball. Continue until everyone on a team has run the course. If kids drop balls, they simply pick them up and keep running.

Once the game is over, discuss with older kids how they may sometimes feel that they're juggling a lot of balls in real life. Talk about how God can help them de-stress their lives.

KOOL-AID QUENCH

Kids learn that Jesus is the "living water."

WHAT YOU'LL NEED:

You'll need a pitcher of Kool-Aid. You might want to choose a flavor that's colorless and stainless such as lemonade. You'll also need a disposable cup for each teammate and a Bible.

ALLERGY ALERT
See page 12.

FOR EXTRA IMPACT:

• Have an extra pitcher of Kool-Aid on hand. Serve with cookies to remind kids of the sweet things Jesus wants to give us.

• Kids can make water paintings to remember that Jesus is the "living water." Have kids each wet a piece of white paper, drip different shades of blue paint (from dark to light) on the wet paper, and watch the colors blend together.

• After the papers have dried, have kids write, "Jesus is the Living Water," on their papers. Then display them in your classroom.

DIRECTIONS

Form two teams. Have each team select a Thirsty Thelma who's given a large cup marked with a fill line. Have teams each form a line with the pitcher of Kool-Aid at one end and their Thirsty Thelma at the other.

Have the first player in each line pour a cup from the pitcher, and then pour it into the next player's cup down the line, headed for Thirsty Thelma.

The first team to fill Thelma's cup to the line and have Thelma drink it wins. If both teams run out of Kool-Aid in the pitcher before they hit the fill line, then the team with the most liquid transported wins.

Afterward, read aloud **John 4:7-26**. Ask: What did Jesus mean when he said he was the "living water"? How does Jesus give us this living water? Why do you think this woman avoided receiving the living water the first time Jesus offered it? How do people keep Jesus from giving them all the good things he wants to? What can you do this week to make sure you have all the good things Jesus wants to give you?

LAZARUS RACE

Kids will love wrapping up this game.

WHAT YOU'LL NEED:

You'll need rolls of toilet paper.

FOR EXTRA IMPACT:

- Read aloud **John 11:1-44,** or paraphrase the story of Lazarus.

- Ask: How do you think all the people felt when they saw Lazarus come out of the tomb? Why do you think Jesus raised Lazarus from the dead?

- Read aloud **John 11:40,** and ask: In what ways can we see God's glory if we believe?

DIRECTIONS

Form four teams. Have each team stand in a circle and pick one person to be Lazarus. Have Lazarus stand in the middle of the circle.

On "go," have each team use one roll of toilet paper to wrap Lazarus. The first team to finish wrapping up Lazarus with the entire roll wins in round one.

Have each Lazarus stand still until all four Lazaruses are wrapped up.

Then call out, "Lazarus, come forth!" The first Lazarus to free him- or herself of all the toilet paper is the winner in round two.

Play as many times as time and toilet paper supplies allow.

LEFT OUT

Kids learn to reach out and include others.

WHAT YOU'LL NEED:

You'll need a Bible and a ball.

FOR EXTRA IMPACT:

- Let kids decide on an act of service they'll do together, such as taking a collection to send to a mission organization or volunteering at a local soup kitchen. Help kids carry out their plan. Ask kids: Why does God want us to reach out to help others?

- Read aloud **Matthew 25:39-40**, and ask: How is our service to others like or unlike serving Jesus?

DIRECTIONS

Form a circle. Have one child stand outside the circle. Give another child in the circle a ball. Have that child pass the ball to someone else in the circle. The outside child tries to tag the child who has the ball. The object of the game is to work together to keep the outside child from tagging the child with the ball. If anyone is tagged, that child becomes the child on the outside of the circle. Or if anyone drops the ball, that child becomes the outside child.

If your group is larger than six, use two players on the outside. Or add two balls and use one outside player.

After this game, have the children sit down. Ask: How did you feel if you were in the circle during this game? on the outside? How are these feelings like or unlike the feelings you have when you leave someone out in real life? when you're left out?

Read aloud **1 John 3:16-18**. Say: God wants us to lovingly include others in our lives. It doesn't feel good to be left out at school or church. Ask: What can we do to include others who are normally left out at school? at church? at home?

Say: Let's pray. God, help us see people who are left out and hurting. Help us welcome them into the things we're doing. Amen.

LINE SWING

Kids will have a swinging good time with this race.

WHAT YOU'LL NEED:

You'll need masking tape and a large gymnasium or outdoor area.

FOR EXTRA IMPACT:

- Read aloud **James 1:5-6**. Have kids read along with you or help kids recite the passage after you. Ask kids: How difficult was it to get to the tape line when you were swinging back and forth? How is that like or unlike when we doubt and don't believe? Why should we ask God for wisdom? How does he help us?

▶ DIRECTIONS

Form teams of no more than eight. For each team, place a masking-tape line the length of your area parallel to each other and about 10 feet apart. Have teams each line up on a masking-tape line at one end of the area, single file and facing the same direction. Have team members link arms.

Say: This race is called Line Swing. The goal is to be the first team to race down to the end of the line and back. But here's the catch: The front person on your team will stand still on the tape. But the rest of the line will swing either to the left or the right until the back person becomes the first person in your line and is standing on the masking tape again. Your team will look like a gate swinging forward. Now the new front person must stay in place while the line swings forward again. Keep swinging your line forward until you get to the end of the line. Then do the same thing coming back.

Play again, but time the teams this time. Challenge your kids to beat the best time during each new round.

LOAVES AND FISHES

Kids learn about Jesus feeding the five thousand.

WHAT YOU'LL NEED:

You'll need clean trash cans, paper wads, cardstock fish or loaves, baskets, spoons, bowls, fish-shaped crackers, and square crackers.

ALLERGY ALERT
See page 12.

FOR EXTRA IMPACT:

- Give kids fish-shaped crackers and saltine crackers to eat for snack as you read aloud **John 6:1-15**. Ask: Why do you think the boy shared his meal? How do you think he felt when he saw the miracle Jesus performed from his offering? Explain. What are things we can offer to God? How can God use our offerings in the lives of others?

DIRECTIONS

Use these two relays when you teach about Jesus feeding the five thousand.

DIGGING FOR DINNER—Form relay teams on one side of the room, and on the other side of the room, fill one clean trash can per team with wadded-up paper. In each team's trash can, hide one cardstock fish or loaf for each child on the team. On "go," have relay teams race across the room, find a fish or loaf, and return to the next person in line until everyone has played.

FILLING BASKETS—Form teams of seven, and give each team a basket, a spoon, and a bowl with two fish-shaped crackers and five square crackers. On "go," have relay teams race across the room with one cracker on a spoon, put the cracker in the basket, and return the spoon to the next person in line until everyone gets a turn.

LOST-COIN HUNT

Kids learn that God rejoices when we repent of our sins.

WHAT YOU'LL NEED:

You'll need a Bible, crayons, a dime for each child, and a flashlight.

FOR EXTRA IMPACT:

- Ask: Why does God rejoice when we repent of our sins?

- Have kids each place their dime under a piece of newsprint or copier paper and carefully rub a crayon on the paper over the dime. Repeat the dime rubbings all over the paper, then write at the top: "God rejoices when we repent!"

- Give kids their dimes to keep in their pockets as reminders that God rejoices when we repent of our sins.

DIRECTIONS

Give each child a different-color crayon and a dime. Have kids each color both sides of their dime.

Collect all the dimes. Turn off the light and close the curtains to make your room dark. Toss the dimes on the floor. Have kids search for their lost coins when you shine the flashlight on the floor. Shine the light several times. Tell kids not to take anyone's coin but their own. The game is over when everyone finds his or her coin.

Turn the light on and read aloud **Luke 15:1-10**. Ask: How did you feel when you lost your coin during this game? How did you feel when you found your coin? How is this game similar to or different from the parable in **Luke 15:1-10**? How does the joy you felt when you found your lost coin compare to the happiness God feels about a sinner who turns back to him?

LOVE TUG

Kids learn about faith sharing.

WHAT YOU'LL NEED:

You'll need a Tug-of-War rope and a handkerchief.

FOR EXTRA IMPACT:

- Have kids play again with only one player on each side. Ask: Was it easier to pull with the team or alone? Explain.

- Give kids each a small piece of white ribbon to tie around their fingers as reminders to ask Jesus to help when they feel pulled in many directions.

- Challenge kids to share their faith in Jesus with someone they know.

DIRECTIONS

Tie a handkerchief in the middle of a Tug-of-War rope. Form evenly matched teams for pulling. Mark off two lines about 3 feet apart in the middle of your playing area. Say: Pretend this handkerchief is someone who doesn't know Jesus. He feels like his life is pulled in many directions.

Have kids try to pull the handkerchief over to their team's side. When one team has accomplished the goal, have them huddle to consider what they might say to the "handkerchief person" to share their faith in Jesus. Play the game several times, making sure both teams have an opportunity to share.

MISSION IMPOSSIBLE

Kids learn that all things are possible with God.

WHAT YOU'LL NEED:

You'll need a Bible and a rope.

FOR EXTRA IMPACT:

- Let kids play again, this time dividing the teams equally. Ask: Which game was more fun? Explain.

- Read aloud **Luke 18:27,** and ask: What does it mean that what's impossible with men is possible with God?

- Have kids tell things that have happened in their lives that would have been impossible without God.

▶ DIRECTIONS

Form two teams. Put stronger children on one team. Then bring out a long rope. Have teams compete in a Tug of War.

Afterward, ask: How did you feel during this game? Was it fair or unfair? Explain.

Paraphrase the story from **1 Samuel 17**. Ask: How do you think David felt when he faced the giant? Was this contest fair or unfair? Explain. How did God help David? What are some giants in your life you must overcome? How can God help you?

NON-MUSICAL CHAIRS

Kids are encouraged to put others ahead of themselves.

WHAT YOU'LL NEED:

You'll need 1 die per 6 children and 1 chair for each child.

FOR EXTRA IMPACT:

• Play a game of Musical Chairs, then have kids compare the two games. Ask: Which game was more like what we are called to do in Scripture? Explain. What are some ways that Jesus put others first?

• Have kids each write a list of things they can do to put others first. Challenge kids to take their lists home and do at least one thing from their list each day. Report back the following week.

DIRECTIONS

Place six chairs in a straight line facing the same direction. If you have more than six children, make several lines of six chairs facing the same direction. Have children each sit in a chair. Then have them number the chairs from one to six.

Roll the die, and call out the number rolled. If you roll a 6, roll again. The child who's sitting in that numbered seat must ask the person in the next higher numbered seat to exchange seats. The person in the higher numbered seat doesn't have to exchange, but the goal of the game is to be sitting in the lowest numbered seat at the conclusion of the game. (Hint: The faster you roll the die, the faster the action will be as kids scramble to get the lowest seat.)

Allow three minutes of die-rolling for each round. At the end of each round, stop and recognize the child occupying the lowest numbered seat in each group.

After the game, read aloud **Philippians 2:3-5**, and discuss how it felt for kids to put others before themselves. Discuss real-life situations where they're required to put others before themselves.

PAPER ATTACK

Kids learn about loyalty.

WHAT YOU'LL NEED:

You'll need newspapers.

FOR EXTRA IMPACT:

- Read aloud **1 Chronicles 29:17-18,** and ask kids: What does it mean to have integrity? Why is it important to keep our hearts loyal to God?

- Have kids find partners and write ways they can be loyal to God. Then have pairs share their lists with the group.

DIRECTIONS

Form teams, and have each team choose a person to be a king or queen. Designate a dividing line down the center of your room. Have teams each stand on a different side of the line with their king or queen standing behind them. Give each person two newspaper wads to throw at the opposing team's royalty. Tell teams to defend their royalty by blocking shots. No one may cross or reach over the center line. Play until a king or queen is hit.

Afterward, ask: Which was more important to you, to hit the opposing royalty or to protect your royalty? Explain. What did it feel like as king or queen to have others defending you? What did loyalty have to do with this game?

PARTNER CARRY

Kids must work together in this cooperative game.

WHAT YOU'LL NEED:

You'll need objects of less than 1 pound.

FOR EXTRA IMPACT:

• Read aloud **Hebrews 12:1,** and ask: How was this game like or unlike the sin that "entangles" as mentioned in the verse? Was it distracting trying to carry the objects with different body parts instead of using your hands? Explain. What are things that entangle us and distract us from our relationship with God? What are things we can do to guard ourselves from distractions so we can persevere in running the race God has set before us?

DIRECTIONS

Form pairs. Have each pair find an object that weighs less than one pound. Then have pairs line up at one end of the room.

Tell partners that when you call out a body part, they must carry that object to the other end of the room and back, using only those body parts.

Call out elbows, knees, ears, foreheads, backs, and shoulders.

PENNY TOSS

Use this game to introduce a lesson on tithing.

WHAT YOU'LL NEED:

You'll need a music player, 2 buckets of pennies, and 2 empty buckets. You'll need 20 pennies for each child. Make 2 lines of masking tape 4 feet apart on the floor.

FOR EXTRA IMPACT:

- Read aloud **2 Corinthians 9:7,** and ask kids: Why does God want us to be cheerful when we give? How do you think God feels when we give? Explain.

- Give each child a paper-covered coffee can to decorate with markers and stickers. Have kids take their cans home and collect change for a designated amount of time.

- Have kids bring the cans back to class and put all the money together. Help kids count the money, then decide which charity the class wants to donate their offering to.

▶ DIRECTIONS

Form two pairs. Have each pair select a Thrower and a Catcher. Have partners stand across from each other on the taped lines. The Catcher on each team holds the empty bucket. The Thrower on each team digs into the penny bucket and tosses as many pennies into the empty bucket as possible in 30 seconds.

Play high-excitement music as the children play. Have the observers cheer while the clock is ticking. Play several rounds of this game.

When the last pairs have played, give each child 20 pennies. Then teach about tithes and offerings from **Malachi 3:8-10**. Children can use their pennies to calculate a tithe.

PETER, JAMES, AND JOHN IN A SAILBOAT

Kids will love this high-energy game of Tag.

WHAT YOU'LL NEED:

Nothing! This is a prop-free, prep-free game.

FOR EXTRA IMPACT:

- Read aloud **Matthew 8:23-27,** and ask kids: Why were the disciples so afraid?

- Have kids tell about times they've been afraid. Ask: What can we do when we're afraid?

- Say: We can trust Jesus to calm our fears, just like he calmed the wind, and waves. Close in prayer, and thank Jesus that he is always by our side.

DIRECTIONS

Choose one player to be the Wind. Form teams of three. Each team has a Peter, James, and John in a sailboat. Team members form a sailboat by standing behind one another and holding the person in front of them around the waist. Team members can sail freely as long as they're in teams of three. Have the Wind chase the sailboats. If the Wind attaches to a sailboat by grabbing the end person's waist, the whole boat tips over. Now all four players chase other teams, trying to tip over their boats. As more players become separated, they may form new sailboats, but never with the same partners. The Wind may also join a sailboat and the "extra" person becomes the Wind.

With smaller groups, you can have two people in a sailboat. Also, the Wind may catch a sailboat and be replaced as the Wind by the first person in the boat.

End the game by portraying Jesus saying, "Peace, be still."

PHARAOH TAG

Kids learn about the Israelites in this fun game of Tag.

WHAT YOU'LL NEED:

You'll need a Bible.

FOR EXTRA IMPACT:

- Have kids make Brick and Mortar Morsels by spreading white icing between graham cracker rectangles.

- As kids eat their snacks, read aloud **Psalm 55:22**. Ask: How can we cast our cares on the Lord? How is the sweetness of our snack like or unlike the sweetness of God's care for us?

See page 12.

DIRECTIONS

Choose a child to be Pharaoh. All the other children will be Israelites. On "go," have Pharaoh tag the Israelites. Whenever Pharaoh tags a child, that child goes into captivity (a corner will work fine). Every now and then, when you yell, "Let my people go!" the captives are set free and Pharaoh gets to choose a new Pharaoh. Continue playing this game until children tire of it.

Afterward, read aloud **Exodus 1:8-14.** Ask: How did it feel to be put in captivity by Pharaoh? How do you think the Israelites felt when they were slaves to the real Pharaoh?

Read aloud **Exodus 3:7-10.** Ask: How did God feel about the Israelites' pain and suffering? How does God help you when you're hurting?

POP! POP!

Kids will have a popping good time with this fun game.

WHAT YOU'LL NEED:

You'll need chairs, tables, and bouncy balls.

FOR EXTRA IMPACT:

- Play again, but this time have kids shout out something they're thankful for each time they put a ball back in the popper. Ask: Was it easier to play the first game or the second game? Explain. Is it easy to remember to thank God each day for all he does for us? Why or why not?

- Read aloud **Psalm 100:4**, and ask: How do you think God feels when we give him thanks and praise? How do you feel when someone thanks you for something you've done?

DIRECTIONS

Mark off a 4x4 area in your room. Create "walls" using chairs and tables around your area. Fill this area with as many bouncy balls as you can—the more the better.

Stand in the area. Tell kids that the balls are like popcorn and are going to pop out of the popper. Their job is to try to put the balls in the popper faster than the balls can pop out.

Start throwing the balls out of the area. After a couple of minutes, choose someone else to be in the popper. Play this game three or four times.

RAINDROP RELAY

Use this game to help kids imagine the great flood.

WHAT YOU'LL NEED:

You'll need 2 buckets per team, a plastic cup for each child, a permanent marker, water, and scissors or a letter opener.

FOR EXTRA IMPACT:

- For a wet and wacky twist, have kids fill large sponges with water, carry the sponges over the heads of their teammates, and squeeze the wet sponges into the buckets.

- Serve kids berry blue Jell-O Jigglers as you read aloud or paraphrase the story of Noah and the flood from **Genesis 7**.

- Fill small water guns with liquid watercolors in assorted rainbow colors. Let kids squirt the paint onto white paper in a rainbow shape to create a unique reminder of God's promise.

See page 12.

DIRECTIONS

Before the game, poke holes on the bottoms and sides of the plastic cups. Draw a line with a permanent marker to indicate the halfway point on both the outside and inside of two buckets.

Form two teams, and have kids sit on the ground in straight lines. Place one bucket filled with water at the front of each line. Place a lined bucket at the back of each line. Then give each child a leaky cup. On "go," have the first child in line fill his or her cup and carry it over the heads of the other kids sitting in line before dumping the remaining water into the bucket at the end of the line. Then the line shifts forward and the cup carrier sits in the back of the line. The game continues until teams fill their back buckets to the halfway marker.

DRY-OFF DEBRIEF: Ask: How did it feel to be constantly rained on during the game? How is this game like or unlike what Noah and his family may have experienced when it rained for 40 days and nights? How do you think Noah and his family felt when they saw God's rainbow?

READY, SET, GO

Kids learn about obedience in this fun relay game.

WHAT YOU'LL NEED:

You'll need 2 sets of the following items: hairbrush, hat, scarf, coat, suitcase, doll, baby bottle, and pillow with pillowcase.

FOR EXTRA IMPACT:

- Play again, but secretly tell one member of each team not to follow any of the directions. Ask: What happens when we don't follow instructions? Explain. How is that like or unlike what happened in our game?

- Read aloud **Deuteronomy 11:1,** and ask kids: Why does God want us to obey his commands?

DIRECTIONS

Form two teams, and have teams line up for a relay race. Lay each set of items at the opposite end of the room on two separate chairs.

On "go," have the first team member run to that team's chair, obey your instruction, and return to the end of his or her team's line.

Call out the following instructions one at a time:

- Brush your hair.
- Put on the hat, scarf, and coat, then take them off.
- Pack clothes in the suitcase.
- Feed a baby with the baby bottle.
- Put the pillowcase on the pillow, then take it off.

Continue playing until all the players have had a turn.

After the game, ask: How did it feel to play this game? How easy or difficult was it for you to follow the instructions? How easy or difficult is it for you to follow your parents' instructions? your teachers'? God's?

ROUNDABOUT RELAY

This wacky relay race will keep kids moving.

WHAT YOU'LL NEED:

You'll need white paper wads and different color paper wads.

FOR EXTRA IMPACT:

- Have kids play again, but this time blindfold the kids or have them close their eyes. Ask: Was it easier playing with the blindfolds on or with your eyes open? Explain.

- Read aloud **Psalm 18:28**. Ask: How does God turn our darkness into light?

DIRECTIONS

Form two teams. Have teams line up across from each other. Give the person in the front of each line a white paper wad. Give the person in the back of each line a different-colored paper wad.

On "go," have the first person in line pass the ball under and through his or her legs to the next person in line. Have the last person in line pass the ball overhead to the person in front of him or her. Have team members continue passing this way until both balls return to their original position.

SCAVENGER HUNT FOR CHARITY

Kids help others with this outreach event.

WHAT YOU'LL NEED:

You'll need 1 adult driver for every 4 kids and a scavenger-hunt food list for each team.

FOR EXTRA IMPACT:

- Give each team a Bible and have someone read aloud **Proverbs 14:31**. Ask teams: How does helping those in need honor God?

- Have teams work together to decorate paper grocery bags with markers, stickers, and ribbons. Let kids find Scripture verses to write on their bags.

- Have teams fill the bags with the food items, then pray for God's blessings on those who'll receive the items.

DIRECTIONS

Form teams of four kids and one adult. Have teams go to homes in the church neighborhood or go in vans to church members' homes. Each team must collect only one food item at each stop. Once all the items are collected, teams meet back at your church. Then donate all the food to a local charity.

The food list per team:
- one can of vegetables,
- one can of fruit,
- one can of soup,
- one cake mix, and
- one box of cereal or other breakfast item.

SEED, SEED, GROW

This game will teach children about growing in their faith.

WHAT YOU'LL NEED:

You'll need a watering can, water, and an outdoor play area.

FOR EXTRA IMPACT:

- Have kids fill plastic cups with crushed Oreo cookies, then plant jelly bean "seeds" in the cookie "dirt." As kids eat the snack, read aloud or paraphrase **Mark 4:26-29**. Ask: How are we like seeds that sprout and grow?

ALLERGY ALERT
See page 12.

- Have kids plant bean seeds in plastic cups filled with potting soil. As kids water and care for the seeds, they can see a visible reminder of how God cares for us so we can grow in him.

DIRECTIONS

This game is a wet version of Duck, Duck, Goose. Have kids sit in a circle on the ground and choose one child to be the Gardener. The Gardener taps kids on the head as he or she says, "Seed!" When the Gardener says, "Grow!" and sprinkles a child's head with the watering can, the Gardener puts down the can and runs from the selected child. If the Gardener is caught, he or she starts over. If the Gardener makes it to the empty spot, the child who was sprinkled gets to be the Gardener.

SHEPHERD AND SHEEP

Kids will love this fun game of Tag.

WHAT YOU'LL NEED:

Nothing! This is a prop-free, prep-free game.

FOR EXTRA IMPACT:

- Ask: Why does a shepherd look after his sheep? What would happen if he didn't?

- Read aloud **Ezekiel 34:11-12**. Ask: How does God look after us?

- Let kids each make a sheep treat by "gluing" miniature marshmallows to a rice cake with white icing. Add a large marshmallow for the head and pretzel sticks for the legs.

See page 12.

DIRECTIONS

Form two teams. Have teams form two lines facing each other in the center of the room. Designate one team as the Shepherds and one team as the Sheep. When the leader calls "sheep," have the Sheep run to tag the Shepherds before they can run to the "safe" wall behind them. If "shepherds" is called, the Shepherds chase the Sheep to their safe wall.

Anyone caught must join the opponent's team. The game continues until all have become Shepherds or Sheep.

To add excitement, draw out the first sound of the team names like this: "shhhhhe-perds!"

SHOE ENOUGH

Kids learn about accepting others.

WHAT YOU'LL NEED:

You'll need a Bible.

FOR EXTRA IMPACT:

- Read aloud **Romans 15:7** and ask: What does it mean to accept others as Christ accepts us? Have you ever been teased or teased someone else? What happened? What would God want us to do if we saw someone being teased?

- Challenge kids not to tease others and to stand up for others when they are teased.

DIRECTIONS

Form pairs. Have partners remove their shoes. Have partners trade shoes, then stand against a wall. On "go," have children each put on their partner's shoes backward and run to the end of the room and back. When kids return, they can trade shoes with their partner to get their own shoes back. Once partners each have their own shoes on, they're finished.

After everyone has finished, have kids sit in a circle. Say: A well-known saying says "Don't judge another person until you've walked a mile in his or her shoes." Ask: What do you think this means? How easy or difficult was it to walk in someone else's shoes?

Read aloud **Matthew 7:1-5.** Ask: What does it mean to judge someone? What does this passage say about judging? Why do you think God doesn't want us to judge others? How have you seen kids judge each other at school? What should we do instead of judging others? How can we "walk a mile" in someone else's shoes?

SHOE-SHOD

Play this game to communicate the value of working together.

WHAT YOU'LL NEED:

Nothing! This is a prop-free, prep-free game.

FOR EXTRA IMPACT:

- Have kids take off their shoes and place them in a pile in the center of the room. On "go," have kids race to find and put on their own shoes.

- Read aloud **1 Corinthians 1:10,** and ask: Why does God want us to work together instead of working against one another? How can we work together in real life?

DIRECTIONS

Have kids line up in teams of six or eight. Have all the children take off their right shoes and place them in a pile at the opposite end of the room. Explain that on "go," the first person in each line will look at the left shoe of the next person in line, then run to find the matching shoe. Each player must bring back the right shoe, put the matching shoe on the second player's foot, and finish fastening it. Players may not accept shoes that aren't theirs. The first player then runs to the end of the line and the second player repeats the process. The first team to have all the shoes back on the right feet and fastened wins.

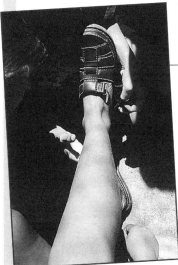

SNAKES ALIVE!

Kids love this game of Tag with a twist.

WHAT YOU'LL NEED:

You'll need masking tape and an activity area.

FOR EXTRA IMPACT:

- Say: In the game, you were tempted to get close to the Snake. Ask: How is that like or unlike temptations we face in life? What are some things that tempt you?

- Read aloud **Mark 14:38,** and ask: What do you think it means that the spirit is willing but the body is weak? How can we be strong and avoid temptation?

DIRECTIONS

Using masking tape, mark off a "garden" area large enough for your kids to run around in, but small enough that they won't have a lot of room. To keep this game safe, have kids wear play clothes and take off their shoes before the fun begins.

Choose the Snake, and have him or her lie on the floor, face down. Have all the other players gather around the Snake and put their hands on the Snake until you say "go."

On "go," set loose the Snake. Kids can run away from it but must stay within the garden. The Snake has to keep its belly on the ground, but it can use any other part of its body to tag kids. Each child touched by the Snake becomes a Snake, too.

Kids will be forced to leap over the Snake or get very close to it. But if the kids step out of the garden, they, too, become Snakes. The last child standing gets to be the first Snake in a new game.

SNEAKER SHUFFLE

Kids learn that God made each of us different.

WHAT YOU'LL NEED:

You'll need a Bible.

FOR EXTRA IMPACT:

- Ask kids: Why do you think God made each of us different?

- Read aloud **1 Corinthians 12:14-31**. Ask: What are some of the different gifts we each have?

- Have kids write a list of specific ways to use their differences to work together as one body and serve God. Hang the list on the wall as a reminder to kids.

DIRECTIONS

Form two teams. Have kids line up single file, facing forward with about 3 feet between each person. The two lines should be directly across from each other. Then have kids each take off their shoes and place them behind their feet.

Say: This is a race. The goal of this race is to be the first team to have all team members wearing their own shoes. Run forward and slip your feet into the shoes of the person in front of you. As soon as your feet are in those shoes as much as possible, take your feet out, run to the next pair and do the same thing. When you get to the front of your team's line, run to the back of the line and start over. Keep doing this until you put your own shoes on. The first team to work its way through the line so every team member is wearing his or her shoes wins.

After the game, read **Psalm 139:13-16** aloud. Then say: God made our feet different from other people's feet. God made each of us different. Ask: What's one wonderful difference about the person in front of you?

Have each child tell one difference.

STOP, THIEF

Kids learn that Jesus is our shepherd.

WHAT YOU'LL NEED:

You'll need a Bible, masking tape, and 20 to 30 cotton balls.

FOR EXTRA IMPACT:

- Ask: What are things in life that steal our time away from Jesus? How is this like or unlike the Robbers in the game?

- Have kids form groups of four and write a list of things they can do each day to spend time with Jesus. Have groups share their lists with the class.

- Have kids choose one action from the list and write it on a piece of paper. Challenge kids to commit to following that action each day.

DIRECTIONS

Mark a large area on the floor with string or masking tape as a sheepfold. Scatter 20 to 30 cotton balls in the sheepfold to represent sheep.

Say: In Bible times, sheep were sometimes kept in a sheepfold surrounded by a stone wall. Sometimes robbers crawled over the wall to steal the sheep. The shepherd chased them away.

Choose a child to be the Shepherd standing inside the sheepfold. The Shepherd can't touch the sheep. Have the other children act as Robbers outside the fold. On "go," the Robbers try to steal the sheep before the Shepherd tags them. When the Shepherd tags a Robber, that Robber is out of the game. The game ends when five Robbers are tagged. When playing again, the first Robber to be tagged becomes the Shepherd.

After playing the game several times, read aloud **John 10:11-16.** Ask: Who are Jesus' sheep? How is Jesus a shepherd for his sheep? Who are the robbers who try to steal away Jesus' sheep? Who are the other sheep who aren't in Jesus' fold yet? Why is Jesus called the good shepherd? How does it feel to know that Jesus is protecting you?

STRENGTH IN NUMBERS

Kids learn that friends can help us be strong in our faith.

WHAT YOU'LL NEED:

You'll need a Bible.

FOR EXTRA IMPACT:

- Let kids have a tug of war with the teams divided unevenly.

- Read aloud **Ecclesiastes 4:12,** and ask: How was this game like or unlike the Scripture verse?

- Give kids each a piece of Twizzlers candy twists as a reminder to be strong in faith with their friends like a chord that's not quickly broken.

ALLERGY ALERT
See page 12.

DIRECTIONS

Choose one child to be "It." Designate a "safe" area in your playing area. On "go," have children run pell-mell around the playing area. When you blow a whistle, children must stop and listen to a number you call out.

After you call out the number, children must race to get in groups of that number. If they're left out of a group, children can run to the safe area. If "It" can tag anyone before he or she joins a group or reaches the safe area, that child becomes "It" for the next game.

After playing this game several times, read aloud **Ecclesiastes 4:9-12.** Ask: What does this Scripture mean? How was there strength in numbers in this game? How does having friends help you be strong in your faith? What are ways we can support each other to help us be strong in our faith at school? home? church?

SUMMER BIBLE OLYMPICS

Get your kids to "go for the gold" with this fun event.

WHAT YOU'LL NEED:

You'll need stick horses decorated with paper donkey ears, tongue depressors, marker, a slingshot, marshmallows, a cardboard "medieval shield," stuffed animals, 2 large boxes, long-handle grabbers (available in most novelty stores) or salad tongs, floral foam painted to resemble birthday cakes, candles, matches, water guns, and lollipops.

FOR EXTRA IMPACT:

• As kids are enjoying their lollipops, ask: How did it feel to win today? to lose? Explain.

• Read aloud **1 Corinthians 15:57,** and say: We may win or lose at games, but we always have victory in Jesus. Ask: Why does God want us to have victory in Jesus?

ALLERGY ALERT
See page 12.

DIRECTIONS

Set up stations for the various games. Kids can rotate through the stations.

RACE TO JERUSALEM—Kids race barefoot around a course on a stick horse with donkey ears. Divide kids into two teams and race against each other.

BIBLE-A-THON—Kids arrange Bible books in order. The books of the Bible are each written on a separate tongue depressor. Have kids work in small groups, pairs, or individually.

DAVID VS. GOLIATH—Kids use a slingshot to hurl marshmallows at a "medieval shield" target. The child who hits the target the most times wins.

NOAH NEEDS HELP—Kids race to see how many stuffed animals they can move from one box to another using a long-handle grabber. (Or use small stuffed animals and salad tongs.)

HAPPY BIRTHDAY, JESUS—Place a lit candle in each floral foam "birthday cake." Let kids race to see who can extinguish the candle first using a water gun.

Give a lollipop to each participant.

TAIL CHASE

Kids learn about unity with others.

WHAT YOU'LL NEED:

You'll need a Bible, a bandanna for each team, pens, and paper.

FOR EXTRA IMPACT:

- Read aloud **Psalm 133:1,** and ask kids: Why is it good and pleasant to live in unity?

- Write the words to **Psalm 133:1** on a bulletin board, and have kids tape their "five secrets to having unity" lists on the board.

- Have kids choose one "secret to unity" from the lists on the board and write it on a sheet of paper. Challenge kids to practice that secret of unity each day.

DIRECTIONS

Form teams of five. Have kids line up with their hands on the waist of the person in front of them. Have the last player tuck a bandanna in his or her pocket or waistband so it hangs out like a tail.

Tell the person at the front of the line to catch the tail. Have the players in the center of the line try to keep the first person from catching the tail. If the line breaks, the person who let go must step aside until the next round. Play for three minutes or until kids catch the tail.

Play the game again, but this time have the kids in the middle of the line help the first person catch the tail.

Afterward, read aloud **Philippians 2:1-2.** Then ask: Which game rules were most like what these verses tell us to do? Explain. What does it mean to be "like-minded"?

Say: Tell about a situation you've experienced where people worked against one another.

With their teams, have kids list five secrets to having unity. After their lists are finished, have kids read them aloud.

Pray: Dear God, help us learn to work together in love. Help us be united. Amen.

THE BEAR

Kids learn that God is our protector.

WHAT YOU'LL NEED:

You'll need a Bible and a teddy bear.

FOR EXTRA IMPACT:

- Read aloud **Deuteronomy 23:14,** and ask kids: Why do you think God protects us?

- Have kids make Bear Bites by mixing together Teddy Grahams and gummy bears. As kids eat the snack, have them tell ways God protects us.

- Teach kids the words to this rhyming prayer:

    Thank you, God, for protecting me,

    In your arms you hold me safely.

See page 12.

DIRECTIONS

Select one child to be the Bear. Have the Bear sit with his or her back to the other children, about 10 to 15 feet away. Put a small stuffed teddy bear behind the back of the Bear. The object of the game is for the Bear to protect the teddy-bear cub while the other children try to take it.

The other children sneak up while the Bear's back is turned. If the Bear hears a person moving, he or she can roar and turn around. If the Bear catches a person moving, that person must go back to the starting line. If no one is caught moving, the Bear turns away from the children again, and play resumes. If a person snatches the cub without the Bear turning around, that person becomes the new Bear.

After the game, read **John 10:28.** Then say: Once you give your life to Jesus, nothing can take you away from him. Even though our cub was snatched away, no one can snatch you away from God.

THE LOST COINS

Kids learn about the parable of the lost coin in this high-energy game.

WHAT YOU'LL NEED:

You'll need a Bible, bales of hay or straw, a large sheet of plastic, and pennies.

FOR EXTRA IMPACT:

- Hide enough pennies in the hay for each child to have one. Let kids each take a penny home as a reminder that God rejoices when we repent of our sins. Ask: Why does God want us to turn away from our sins and follow him? What can we do to help us remember to look to God?

- Close with this prayer: Help me, God, to turn from my sins and follow you each day. When I do, you will rejoice because I follow your way. In Jesus' name, amen!

DIRECTIONS

Beforehand, spread out one or two bales of hay on the grass. If you'll play this game inside, place the hay on a large sheet of plastic. Sprinkle several pennies into the hay, and toss the hay around. If you don't have access to hay or straw, use shredded paper, packing peanuts, or mud.

When children arrive, encourage them to search through the hay to find the lost coins. Whenever a child finds a coin, lead all the children in celebrating.

After all the coins have been found or children tire of this game, read aloud the parable of the lost coin from **Luke 15:8-10.** Ask children to compare their experience and feelings in searching for the coins to the story from Scripture.

THREE-LEGGED TREASURE HUNT

Kids will love this game created by 9-year-old Jordan Sharp.

WHAT YOU'LL NEED:

You'll need candy, a timer, and 1 bandana or tie and 1 blindfold for each pair of kids.

ALLERGY ALERT
See page 12.

FOR EXTRA IMPACT:

- As kids eat the candy, have them tell about sweet things in their lives, such as reading a book with Mom or Dad or playing with friends.

- Read aloud **Psalm 119:103**, and ask kids: How do God's words sweeten our lives?

- Have kids tape a piece of candy to a card with the words of **Psalm 119:103** written on it. Encourage kids to give the cards away as reminders of the sweetness of God's Word.

DIRECTIONS

Hide pieces of candy throughout a large room or gym. Form pairs. Tie the partners' ankles together so the pair is three-legged. Blindfold one child in each pair. Set a timer for two minutes, and have the pairs hunt for the candy. When time is up, have the other partner in each pair wear the blindfold. Set the timer for two minutes, and have pairs hunt again for the remaining candy.

TRASH-BAG BONANZA

Use a plastic trash bag instead of a ball for a wacky game alternative.

WHAT YOU'LL NEED:

You'll need 32-gallon trash bags, Hula-Hoops, packing tape, and quarters.

FOR EXTRA IMPACT:

- Have kids form two teams, and give each team a twin sheet. Teams toss the trash-bag ball back and forth using the sheets as nets to catch the ball.

- Choose three kids to be "It," and give them each a trash-bag ball. Then have a wild and wacky game of Dodgeball with all three balls in play.

- Let kids play a game of Jumbo Badminton by using tennis rackets and trash-bag balls. You can use a rope tied between two trees if you don't have a net available.

DIRECTIONS

Swish an open 32-gallon trash bag through the air, tightly twist the opening, and seal it with packing tape. The bag will hold air for five to 30 minutes. Then play these fun games.

TRASHKETBALL—Form two teams, and give each team a Hula-Hoop plastic hoop. Have one goalie per team hold a hoop "goal" horizontally. The goalies should stand 8 feet apart. The goalies can move sideways to catch the ball for their team, but they can't move forward.

Start the game with a "toss-off" by tossing the ball into the air. The first child to touch the ball volleys it to a team member who then volleys it to another team member as they try to score a goal. Team members can't hold the ball, and it must remain in the air. The other team tries to intercept the ball and score its own goal. If the ball hits the ground or a goal is scored, play again with another toss-off.

UPKEEP—Tape a quarter to a trash-bag ball with a piece of packing tape. The quarter causes the ball to move in an unpredictable direction. Have kids see how many consecutive times they can toss the ball into the air without it touching the ground.

TWO-SPOON BALLOON RACE

This wild game is fun when the balloons start flying in all directions.

WHAT YOU'LL NEED:

You'll need 2 spoons and an inflated balloon for each team.

FOR EXTRA IMPACT:

- For a fun twist, have two teammates race to the finish line side by side, each using one spoon to bat the balloon back and forth to each other.

- Have kids hold their own spoons in their teeth and balance the balloons on the spoons without using their hands. Kids each slowly walk down the relay line without dropping the balloon, then pass it from their spoon onto their teammates' spoon without using their hands.

DIRECTIONS

Form two teams or more. Teams should have equal numbers of kids. Have the teams line up for a relay race. Give each team two spoons and an inflated balloon.

Teams race by having teammates hold a spoon in each hand and only touch the team's balloon with the spoons. Each teammate must run in this way to the end of the room, return, and pass off the spoons and balloon. Continue until every player has had a turn.

WATER FIGHT

Kids will love this wet and wild game!

WHAT YOU'LL NEED:

You'll need 2 pairs of goggles, 4 squirt bottles, a bucket of water, 2 mats, and 2 cans of shaving cream.

FOR EXTRA IMPACT:

- Let kids move balloons across a finish line by squirting the balloons with water guns.

- Have kids form teams and give each team a squirt bottle, a sponge, and a cup. Teams fill up their cups by squirting their sponges with water and squeezing them into the cup.

DIRECTIONS

Form two teams. Have the first person in each team kneel on a mat, with the team members lined up behind him or her. Give each kneeling child a pair of goggles and a water-filled squirt bottle. Have them put on their goggles. Spray a dab of shaving cream on each child's chin.

Then on "go," have kids use their bottles to spray the shaving cream off each other's chin. Once all the shaving cream is gone, that child can hand off his or her bottle and goggles to the next person in line. Any child who still has shaving cream on his or her chin when a new child begins to play on the other team must stay until all the shaving cream is gone. Refill the extra squirt bottles as children play so you always have two full squirt bottles on hand.

Continue until everyone has had a chance to play—even if it means having some kids play twice so others can have a turn.

WEB OF FRIENDS VOLLEYBALL

Kids learn about the importance of supporting one another.

WHAT YOU'LL NEED:

You'll need yarn, tape, a volleyball, and a net.

FOR EXTRA IMPACT:

- Write the word *burdens* on several inflated balloons. As kids hold onto the yarn web, have them use the web as a net and bounce the balloons back and forth.

- Read aloud **Galatians 6:2,** and ask kids: What does it mean to carry each other's burdens? How was batting the balloons like or unlike supporting our friends and bearing their burdens?

- Have younger kids play the game by sitting in a circle and rolling the yarn ball back and forth. Have the child who catches the ball say something kind about the child he or she received the ball from, hold onto a piece of the yarn, then roll the ball to another child.

▶ DIRECTIONS

Before this game, tape one end of a skein of yarn to a volleyball. Wrap the entire skein around the ball, leaving the other end free. Set up a net, or string a rope across the room about 5 feet high.

Form two teams. Have a server on one team hold the end of the yarn and volley the ball across the net. The player who catches the ball on the other side holds the yarn and volleys the ball back to the other side. Continue playing until players reach the end of the yarn.

Afterward, discuss how this web of Christian friends can support one another no matter how tangled life may become.

WISE AND FOOLISH MAIDENS

Kids learn to be ready and watch for Jesus.

WHAT YOU'LL NEED:

You'll need a Bible.

FOR EXTRA IMPACT:

• Ask kids: What did you think when you were left out of the wedding circle? How was that like or unlike the way the maidens might've felt when they weren't allowed in the wedding banquet? Why does Jesus want us to be ready and wait for him like the 10 wise maidens?

• Have kids frost and decorate a "wedding" cake. As kids eat the snack, ask them to tell ways we can be prepared and watch for Jesus.

See page 12.

DIRECTIONS

Choose five Wise Maidens and a Bridegroom. Have the Bridegroom crouch on the floor with his or her eyes closed. The Wise Maidens form the wedding circle around the Bridegroom, hold hands, and raise their arms.

The rest of the children are Foolish Maidens, traveling outside the circle and looking for oil. While the arms of the Wise Maidens are raised, the Foolish Maidens may search inside the wedding circle for their oil. But they must keep moving in and out of the circle.

When the Bridegroom stands, the Wise Maidens' arms fall and trap some lucky Foolish Maidens inside the circle. The rest are left out. Those trapped inside become part of the wedding circle for the next round. Continue play until there are 10 maidens in the wedding circle.

Afterward, read aloud and discuss **Matthew 25:1-13.**

YOU ARE SPECIAL

Kids learn about the importance of encouraging others.

WHAT YOU'LL NEED:

You'll need 5 construction-paper "tickets" for each child.

FOR EXTRA IMPACT:

- Ask: What was your reaction when others were saying special things about you? What was it like to say nice things to others? Explain.

- Read aloud **1 Thessalonians 5:11,** and ask: Why does the Scripture verse tell us to encourage one another? What happens when we are supportive and encouraging to others?

- Have kids write the words of **1 Thessalonians 5:11** on a sheet of construction paper. Then tape several "special" tickets on the papers to take home as reminders to encourage others.

DIRECTIONS

Give kids each five "special" tickets. You can make these by writing "special" on ticket-like pieces of construction paper. On "go," have kids race to get rid of all their special tickets. To get rid of one of their special tickets, kids must each find one other person, tell one thing that's special about themselves and one thing that's special about that person. Once they do, they can give one special ticket to that person. Continue playing until kids' original five tickets are given away.

Afterward, say: You've given away all your special tickets, but you got new ones. We've got some pretty special people in our group.

YOU'RE OUT

Kids learn to include others in what they do.

WHAT YOU'LL NEED:

You'll need balloons in 5 different colors, enough for each child to have 1 balloon. You'll also need index cards, a bag, crayons, a praise music CD or cassette, and a player.

FOR EXTRA IMPACT:

• Read aloud **Colossians 3:12,** and ask kids: What does it mean to clothe yourself with compassion and kindness?

• Have kids work together to write a list of ways they can show compassion and kindness to others.

• Challenge kids to pick one action from the list to do during the week. Let kids report back the next week.

DIRECTIONS

Inflate and tie off enough balloons for each child to have one. Color one index card to match each balloon color, and put the cards into a bag.

Play bouncy praise music. Say: While the music is playing, bop the balloons to keep them in the air. When the music stops, catch a balloon and hold it. Then I'll put my hand into this bag and pull out a card. If you're holding a balloon that's the color of the card, you're out.

Return the cards each time to the bag and keep all the balloons in play. Kids who are "out" need to sit along the wall. Play four times. Then ask: How did it feel to have the "you're out" color? How does it feel to be left out of something your friends are doing? How do kids exclude others from playing games? from being their friends? What do you think Jesus thinks when we treat people unkindly and leave them out? How might Jesus change this game?

Play the game again with the kids' Jesus-style rules. Ask: Did changing the rules make the game more fun or less fun? How can we change the "game rules" in our lives so we do what Jesus wants when we see others being left out?

ZIGZAG RELAY

Kids will love this fast-paced game!

WHAT YOU'LL NEED:

You'll need 2 balls of clay.

FOR EXTRA IMPACT:

- Read aloud **1 Corinthians 6:19-20.** Ask: What does it mean that your body is the temple of the Holy Spirit?

- Ask: How can we honor God with our bodies?

- Give each person a small lump of clay to take home. Remind kids to honor God with their bodies.

▶ DIRECTIONS

Form two teams, and have each team line up. Give the team member in the front of each line a ball of clay.

On "go," have the first teammate pass the clay ball backward between his or her legs to the next teammate. Have the next teammate pass the clay backward over his or her head. Continue passing the clay over and under to the end of the line.

When the clay reaches the last teammate, that person runs to the front and restarts the passing exercise. When the original first teammates return to the front of their lines, the game is over.

Afterward, have kids sit in a circle on the floor. Ask: How did the clay look at the end of the game compared to how it looked at the beginning? What are some negative things that can push our bodies out of shape? (Kids might answer eating junk food, using drugs, drinking alcohol, or smoking.) How can bad habits change the way our bodies look and work?

After your discussion, close in prayer, thanking God for healthy bodies.

THE BEST OF

children's
ministry
MAGAZINE

GAMES

SCRIPTURE
INDEX

OLD TESTAMENT

INDEX

INDEX

INDEX

INDEX